Testing in Software Development

# THE BRITISH COMPUTER SOCIETY MONOGRAPHS IN INFORMATICS

Editor: Professor P. A. Samet

Monographs in Informatics contain reports from BCS members and specialist groups. The series publishes new research material and assesses recent developments in a broad range of computer topics. Through the Monographs in Informatics series computer scientists are able to share the specialist knowledge of members of the Society, and at the same time keep abreast of current research.

Some current titles:

Buying Financial Accounting Software
BCS Auditing by Computer Specialist Group

Buying Payroll Software
BCS Auditing by Computer Specialist Group

Practical PL/I
G. R. Clarke, S. Green and P. Teague

Database Design: A Classified and Annotated Bibliography
M. Agosti

Testing in Software Development
BCS Working Group on Testing
Eds. M. A. Ould and C. Unwin

# Testing in Software Development

Members of the British Computer Society Working Group on Testing

*Edited by*
Martyn A Ould (Praxis Systems plc) **and Charles Unwin** (Logica Financial Systems Ltd)

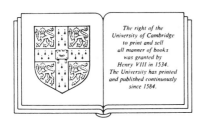

The right of the
University of Cambridge
to print and sell
all manner of books
was granted by
Henry VIII in 1534.
The University has printed
and published continuously
since 1584.

*Published by*
CAMBRIDGE UNIVERSITY PRESS
*on behalf of*
THE BRITISH COMPUTER SOCIETY
*Cambridge*
*London New York New Rochelle*
*Melbourne Sydney*

Published by the Press Syndicate of the University of Cambridge
The Pitt Building, Trumpington Street, Cambridge CB2 1RP
32 East 57th Street, New York, NY 10022, USA
10 Stamford Road, Oakleigh, Melbourne 3166, Australia

First published 1986

Printed in Great Britain at the
University Press, Cambridge

British Library cataloguing in publication data
Testing in software development - (British Computer Society
    monographs in informatics)
    1. Computer software - Development
    I. British Computer Society. *Working Group on Testing.*
    II. Ould, Martyn A. III. Unwin, Charles IV. Series

    005.1        QA76.76.D47

Library of Congress CIP data available

ISBN 0 521 33786 0

# Contents

*Preface*

1   Introduction                                                            1

2   The Manager's View of Testing                                           4

    2.1   The need to manage testing                                        4
          2.1.1   Management's role                                         4
          2.1.2   Why are there errors in software?                         5
          2.1.3   Three key ideas                                           5
          2.1.4   An eight-point programme for managers                     6
    2.2   A model of the software development process                       6
    2.3   The four views of testing                                        8
          2.3.1   Introduction                                              8
          2.3.2   The manager's view                                        9
          2.3.3   The user's view                                          10
          2.3.4   The designer's view                                      10
          2.3.5   The programmer's view                                    11
    2.4   System development and testing                                   11
          2.4.1   Introduction                                             11
          2.4.2   Static testing                                           11
          2.4.3   Dynamic testing                                          13
          2.4.4   Testability                                              16
          2.4.5   Verification and validation                              17
          2.4.6   Translating the life-cycle diagram into a project plan   18
    2.5   Change management                                                19
          2.5.1   Configuration management                                 19
          2.5.2   Change control                                           20
          2.5.3   Version control                                          21
          2.5.4   Record-keeping and traceability                          21
    2.6   Special management concerns in testing                           22
          2.6.1   Educating staff                                          22
          2.6.2   Contractual requirements and testing objectives          23
          2.6.3   Establishing a budget for testing                        23
          2.6.4   Planning the tests                                       24
          2.6.5   Establishing a method                                    25

| | | | |
|---|---|---|---|
| | 2.6.6 | Starting early | 25 |
| | 2.6.7 | Testing through the life of the system | 26 |
| | 2.6.8 | Measurement and data collection | 26 |

**3    The User's View of Testing**    28

| | | | |
|---|---|---|---|
| 3.1 | | Introduction | 28 |
| 3.2 | | Testing the Requirements Expression | 30 |
| | 3.2.1 | Introduction | 30 |
| | 3.2.2 | Criteria for testing a Requirements Expression | 31 |
| | 3.2.3 | Techniques for testing a Requirements Expression | 37 |
| 3.3 | | Testing the System Specification | 41 |
| | 3.3.1 | Introduction | 41 |
| | 3.3.2 | How does one test a System Specification? | 41 |
| | 3.3.3 | Qualifying a System Specification | 41 |
| | 3.3.4 | Validating a System Specification | 46 |
| | 3.3.5 | The ideal form of a System Specification | 52 |
| 3.4 | | Testing the System for Trial | 53 |
| | 3.4.1 | Introduction | 53 |
| | 3.4.2 | The Acceptance Test | 54 |
| | 3.4.3 | Testing functional statements | 54 |
| | 3.4.4 | Testing constraints | 55 |
| | 3.4.5 | Testing attributes | 56 |
| | 3.4.6 | The format of an Acceptance Test Plan | 56 |
| | 3.4.7 | Testing an Acceptance Test | 57 |

**4    The Designer's View of Testing**    59

| | | | |
|---|---|---|---|
| 4.1 | | The system design process | 59 |
| 4.2 | | Testing the design | 61 |
| | 4.2.1 | What to test for in a system design | 61 |
| | 4.2.2 | Test methods for a system design | 63 |
| 4.3 | | Integration testing | 69 |
| | 4.3.1 | Introduction | 69 |
| | 4.3.2 | The scope of integration | 71 |
| | 4.3.3 | The objectives of integration | 71 |
| | 4.3.4 | The organisation of integration | 72 |
| | 4.3.5 | The Integration Test Plan | 73 |
| | 4.3.6 | Integration Test Specifications | 75 |
| | 4.3.7 | Test software | 79 |
| 4.4 | | System testing | 82 |

**5      The Programmer's View of Testing**                                   88

5.1      Introduction                                                         88
5.2      Testing the Module Specification                                     89
         5.2.1      Introduction                                              89
         5.2.2      Testing the quality of the Module Specification           90
         5.2.3      Verification of the Module Specification                  96
5.3      Testing the Unit Test Plan                                           97
         5.3.1      Introduction                                              97
         5.3.2      Checking the quality of the Unit Test Plan                97
         5.3.3      Requirements-directed generation of test data             97
         5.3.4      Design-directed generation of test data                   99
5.4      Unit testing                                                        103
         5.4.1      Introduction                                             103
         5.4.2      Checking the quality of coded units                      103
         5.4.3      Verification of coded units                              109
         5.4.4      Supporting techniques                                    111

*Bibliography*                                                              113

*Index*                                                                    118

# Preface

The British Computer Society Working Group on Testing first met as a number of people who shared an interest in the topic of software testing. After a few meetings it became clear that there was common agreement that testing was something that should take place throughout the development of software. Most software developers probably feel this is true but emphasis has too often been given to the testing of *code*. In order to redress the balance the Working Group felt that a book that gave equal emphasis to testing at *every* stage of development would be useful to the software engineering community.

This book is therefore an attempt to show how every step of development is a step at which some form of testing can be done. In a slim volume on a topic that is itself fast-moving we can only hope to show the reader what possibilities there are. Advances in formal methods and in theoretical work, together with the increasing availability of computer-based tools make this more so. As always the real improvements in testing must come from personal study of the techniques, knowledge of the tools and *practice*.

The following members of the Working Group contributed to this book under the chairmanship of Patrick Hall:

Barry Bird (Scicon Ltd)
Gary Born (Systems Designers)
Geoff Cozens (Burroughs Machines Limited)
Gillian Frewin (STL)
Mike Gardner (Rolls-Royce plc)
Chris Gerrard (Advanced Software Consultants Ltd)
Patrick Hall (Cirrus Computers)
Barbara Hatton (STL)
Phil Kenyon (Plessey Electronic Systems Research Ltd)
Tony Mounter (STL)
Martyn Ould (Praxis Systems plc)
Geoff Quentin (Keith London Associates)
Marc Roper (Sunderland Polytechnic)
Charles Unwin (Logica Financial Systems Ltd).

We would like to record our thanks to Sandie Earnshaw at Praxis Systems for help in the preparation of the camera-ready copy, and to the Directors of Praxis Systems for the use of preparation facilities. The editors would also like to thank Jack Bowles of Cambridge University Press for the professional advice he gave to them as amateur book designers; whilst the book in no way lives up to his high standards its appearance was much improved by his comments. Finally, the book and the activities of the Working Group would not be possible without the kind permission of our respective employers and the provision of meeting facilities by the British Computer Society.

All the opinions expressed are those of the authors and are not necessarily those of their employers or the British Computer Society.

The meanings of terms used in this book are given in the text rather than in a separate glossary; the Index can be used to trace such terms. Items of literature listed in the Bibliography are referred to in the text by the name of the first author and the year of publication, for instance [Myers 1979].

*Martyn Ould and Charles Unwin (editors)*
*June 1986*

# Chapter 1 - Introduction

The testing of software is a practice as long established as that of developing software itself. But it has generally been seen as a secondary activity, something done afterwards to confirm that the correct software has been built. Executing the software after its initial production, during a test or integration phase, may take as much or even more effort than the development of the software up to that point. And the consequences of putting faulty software into service can be catastrophic. The computer industry abounds with stories of mistakes. As computers and computer systems play an increasingly dominant role in the lives of everyone, the chance of their involvement in disasters is becoming more likely. Defective computer systems have already contributed to the loss of aircraft, the collapse of bridges, false nuclear alerts, the collapse of businesses, and so on. Many of the defects have been in the software: a space probe was lost because of a transcription error in keying in a FORTRAN program; a centralised computer facility for vehicle and driving licence records aimed at saving costs over a previous distributed manual system is in the end many times more expensive; and customers have received gas bills for £0.00.

The computing industry has responded by devoting a lot of effort to improving the methods used for producing software, from Structured Programming and Structured Analysis and Design, through to the use of mathematically based formal methods. All these endeavours are aimed at spending more care and attention before the production of code, aimed in effect at "getting it right first time", or at least less wrong.

In all these software production methods there comes a strong element of testing - not only testing in the sense of exercising the code using examples, but also testing in the sense of making some development step and then reflecting on the results of the step to check whether they were really what was intended. It is interesting to observe how testing was at one time thought of as simply a process of exercising code with a number of test cases. With the advent of *semi-formal* methods of systems analysis and design such as Jackson Structured Programming (JSP) and Structured System Analysis and Design Methodology (SSADM) there came the possibility of bringing forward testing into the analysis and design phases of development and testing statements of requirement and design rather than waiting until the code had been written before carrying out any sort of test. The more recent arrival of *formal* (ie mathematically based) methods such as VDM and Z strengthens this possibility even further. This is a much wider view of testing than the traditional one, but it is one that is being increasingly adopted.

We adopt this broad view of testing here: testing is viewed as an integral part of the software development process which takes place at *all* stages, a continual assessment of whether the software being produced will meet the needs of the users. Testing embraces a wide spectrum of activities ranging from informal design reviews, through rigorous test case analysis to formal proofs of correctness. Moreover, in any method that we use to develop software we should expect to find provision for testing each development step. A "good" method is one that comes with testing built in and it is important to understand that testing is an essential part of any development method - not an add-on. (For a description of current development methods including how they can assist in testing see for example [Birrell 1985].)

Rather than focus on a particular sequence of steps during development of the software - a life-cycle - we have focussed on four views of the life-cycle, four different concerns within software development. These are:

- *Management*: the continuous assessment of the correctness of the software must be made a cornerstone of the development process. This can only occur if management establishes projects with testing in mind from the outset and then takes corrective action throughout development.

- *User*: the users of the system are concerned that the system that is being developed is appropriate to their needs, and are particularly active during the early stages when their requirements are being analysed and the system is being specified or prototyped, and in the final stages when the system undergoes formal acceptance tests and trial use.

- *Designer*: the system must be feasible, and specified unambiguously, and then transformed into a design of software decomposed into interacting components that together will provide the functions required. Once the components have been produced, they must be integrated and tested to confirm that they do implement the design. Testing that these activities have been done correctly is the concern of the system's designer.

- *Programmer*: component specifications must be transformed into program code that meets those specifications. The component design must be tested to see that it conforms with the specification, and later the code must be exercised to check that it does indeed implement the specification. These are the stages where responsibility for testing falls on the programmer.

The basic techniques, especially those relating to the later stages of development where the software itself is exercised, are extensively described in standard texts such as [Myers 1979], [Beizer 1983], [Beizer 1984] and [Hetzel 1984] and the reader is referred to these for greater detail. In this book we have outlined the techniques and tried to set them in the larger context which includes the testing of specifications - an area that is currently less well treated in the literature.

2

Naturally in a book of this size we can only look at the aspects of testing that apply to the majority of software developments in the industry and we do not have the room to cover testing techniques specific to particular types of system. However, we do point out development methods that give strong support to testing and we give references to the relevant literature. Also, the bias of the book is towards the development of a system for a user, rather than of a product for a market; however, with appropriate translation of terms and senses much of the book can be usefully translated into this important arena.

Tool support is an important consideration for any method. In some instances we note tools that are available at the time of writing but this is an area where the market changes rapidly so we do not attempt in any way to be exhaustive. However, in the UK *The STARTS Guide* [NCC 1984] produced by the NCC and the Department of Trade and Industry includes useful coverage of tools for software testing, and similar publications are available in the USA from, for instance, the National Bureau of Standards.

Some testing techniques and concepts can be used at several stages of development. How they are used varies according to the development product they are being used on so such methods will be found to be mentioned several times.

Finally, in a book on testing it is not unreasonable to expect to find a definition of the term. But rather than give a one-liner that might sound wise but is of little practical use, we believe that the most useful definition is that

*software testing is at least the activities described in this book.*

# Chapter 2 - The Manager's View of Testing

## 2.1    The need to manage testing

This chapter presents the management view of testing. However, it is intended not only for project managers but for all staff involved in all stages of software production. Therefore, we suggest that you at least skim all the chapters to see what material is relevant to you and that, whatever your particular interest, you start by reading this chapter since it presents the fundamental concepts for all views of testing.

After this introductory section in which we discuss the importance of management to good testing, we present the model of the development life-cycle. From this we derive the perspective taken in this book, which is to regard testing from four viewpoints: the manager's, the user's, the designer's and the programmer's. Configuration Management is an essential concept for testing and is given a section of its own. The chapter concludes with a discussion of special management concerns in testing.

### 2.1.1    Management's role

Testing needs to be done at each stage of software development from problem statement through to implementation and even into post-implementation evaluation. If testing is not done adequately then disasters can occur. It is a vital but regrettably underestimated process in the development of computer systems.

The longer that defects are left in the development process, the more expensive it is to remove them. The results of insufficient testing are delayed projects and cost overruns. It is clear that there has to be far more effort put into testing. These concerns are the responsibility of management.

It is important to realise that with the techniques currently available to us the process of developing and maintaining computer systems is bound to allow defects or errors might occur. It is the responsibility of the software engineering professional to realise this and to work to prevent such defects as far as possible (this is the purpose of good *methods*), and to eliminate defects immediately should they enter the development process. The emphasis should be on *fault management* and *defect removal*.

*The manager's role in adopting this approach to faults is vital.* It is the manager's decisions that bring about the move towards higher quality and defect-free products.

## 2.1.2    Why are there errors in software?

Errors enter into software development because of problems in translation: systems analysts do not correctly translate user requirements into requirements documents, designers do not correctly translate requirements into designs and programmers do not correctly translate designs into program code. The job of testing is to discover and remove these errors as early as possible in the development cycle.

Studies consistently show that testing is poorly understood and insufficiently carried out. During a training course on testing that was given to well over a thousand experienced analysts and programmers in the United Kingdom, it was found that:

- They considerably underestimated the number of tests required to verify a straightforward program - typically, they thought of only a third of the required number of tests.
- Only about ten per cent had the persistence and accuracy of observation to detect all the errors in a sample of code during desk checking.
- When they were asked to review a piece of logic with the objective of analysing style, only about one per cent observed defects not related to style.

Very experienced programmers were found in one study to make one error in every 30 lines of code, with inexperienced programmers performing far less well.

The situation is clear: testing has to be done, it has to be organised, it has to have an adequate budget, and staff have to be trained to apply a methodical approach. This is a matter for management.

## 2.1.3    Three key ideas

There are three key ideas that we will use throughout this book:

- deliverables
- the recording of test results
- a life-cycle approach.

A *deliverable* or *end product* is the result of a development activity: for instance, a Module Specification document is the end product of a detailed design activity. End products are at the centre of thorough testing methods. An end product must be identified and defined for every activity.

The output of tests should also be treated as an end product and stored as proof of testing. It can become very important after the system is delivered if litigation should ensue. Testing is an assurance that what has been produced has been produced correctly. Staff must be trained to *record the results of tests* as testing proceeds; this might mean changing or adapting practical techniques to allow far more inspection and testing on intermediate end products.

The *life-cycle approach* to software development described in section 2.2 provides a framework for testing. It defines all the end products within the project and the activities needed to produce them. It creates a framework for all end products and then for testing them as they are produced.

## 2.1.4 An eight-point programme for managers

In the following table we recommend a programme of actions for management who are responsible for the development of software.

*An eight-point action plan for managers*

| | |
|---|---|
| 1 | educate staff toward defect removal |
| 2 | set up an organisation for testing |
| 3 | set objectives for testing and product quality |
| 4 | establish an adequate budget |
| 5 | plan the testing process |
| 6 | establish a methodical approach to testing |
| 7 | ensure that testing is started early |
| 8 | continue testing throughout the life of the product |

## 2.2 A model of the software development process

As practical methods for developing software have evolved, the concept of the *life-cycle* has come into prominence. Since each software project is different, it is impossible to specify a general life-cycle model and a number of different life-cycles have been proposed. However, for many of the systems that are encountered in the industry today, the traditional *waterfall model* is appropriate to the methods and tools available and it can be adapted to specific project needs. In this model system development is divided into a number of phases each of which has identifiable activities and end products. There are also well-defined links between the end products and these are used as the basis for the various testing activities described in this book. Our generic model has eight "typical" phases and is shown in its simplest form (ignoring iteration) in figure 2.1.

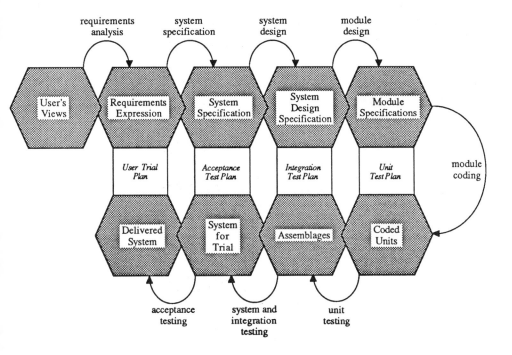

Figure 2.1 - The generic life-cycle model

This diagram is used as the basis for the book. The life-cycle model contains eight life-cycle activities. They are represented (as in subsequent diagrams) by arrows. At their tails are hexagons representing the deliverables that form their inputs; at their heads are the deliverables that form their outputs. The activities are:

- requirements analysis
- system specification
- system design
- module design
- module coding (programming)
- unit testing
- integration and system testing
- acceptance testing.

7

The upper activities running in chronological order from left to right are *specification* activities; their deliverables describe what some other thing should do or be like. The lower activities running from right to left are *implementation* activities; their deliverables are produced to satisfy their counterpart specifications.

The eight deliverables linking these activities appear in the diagrams as shaded hexagons. They are:

- Requirements Expression
- System Specification
- System Design Specification
- Module Specifications
- Coded Units
- Assemblages
- System for Trial
- Delivered System.

There are four Test Plans, each of which is itself an end product linking a specification deliverable to an implemented deliverable:

- User Trial Plan
- Acceptance Test Plan
- Integration Test Plan
- Unit Test Plan.

As mentioned earlier, testing a system against the user's expectations is outside the scope of this book so we do not cover the User Trial Plan further, but include it here for completeness.

## 2.3    The four views of testing

### 2.3.1    Introduction

From our life-cycle model we can identify four views of testing corresponding to vertical "slices" through the model as illustrated in figure 2.2:

- management's view
- the user's view
- the designer's view
- the programmer's view.

8

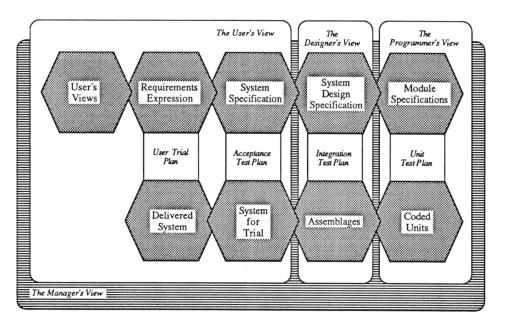

Figure 2.2 - The four views of testing

It is important to realise that these are only different ways of viewing the same process. In most cases, there is a significant overlap between viewpoints. Also, on many projects, staff are required to take on one or more of these roles. Indeed, on small projects, one person may take on all four roles!

We now go on to outline each of the different views in turn, leaving it to subsequent chapters to look in detail at the testing activities that are of interest to each group.

## 2.3.2    The manager's view

The management view of testing emphasises structure, organisation, planning and control:

- *structure*: the life-cycle concept and the phases of testing; the relationships between the activities and deliverables within a software project
- *organisation*: how testing and the people involved are organised

- *planning*: how and when to plan testing activities; defining the deliverables
- *control*: configuration management, change control and version control; the control of quality with test methods; the early detection of errors through verification techniques; measurement and data collection.

### 2.3.3   The user's view

The emphasis here is on ensuring that the system meets the user's requirements: in other words on defining those requirements clearly and then ensuring that they are embodied in the final system. The book covers:

- *Requirements Analysis*: capturing the user's requirements (systems analysis), documenting them in the Requirements Expression and verifying that that document is an accurate representation of the requirements
- *System Specification*: defining the functions and attributes of a system that satisfies the requirements and structuring them in a way suitable for implementation on a computer
- *Acceptance Testing* and the *Acceptance Test Plan*: verifying that the delivered computer system meets the user requirements as expressed in the System Specification; using the Acceptance Test Plan to plan this form of testing; confirming that the system is ready for delivery to users.

### 2.3.4   The designer's view

The emphasis in this viewpoint is on the difficult task of converting the user- and function-orientated documents of the user's view into a design for the system. It covers:

- *System Design*: designing the software for the system, with emphasis on its architecture and the interfaces between the components
- *System Design Specification*: documenting the results of the system design process; verification of the document using the System Specification
- *Integration and System Testing* and the *Integration Test Plan*: testing that the components of the system correctly combine to form a complete system of subsystems; testing that interfaces between components are correct; confirming that the system is ready for Acceptance Testing.

## 2.3.5    The programmer's view

This viewpoint emphasises the development of the system in terms of the software components - *modules* - designed and coded by programmers. It covers not only the "bugs" that may enter the coding process but also elements of design and the structure of the code:

- *Module Specification*: determining the required functionality and properties of each module (the *what*); verifying them against the System Design Specification
- *Module Design*: designing a module to meet its specification (the *how*)
- *Module Coding*: producing the source code that implements the chosen design
- *Unit Testing* and the *Unit Test Plan*: testing that a module correctly implements its design and is ready to be integrated into the subsystem or full system; preparation of Test Plans for modules.

## 2.4    System development and testing

### 2.4.1    Introduction

In every form of testing we compare one deliverable with another: specification with specification, or implementation with specification. All testing ultimately concerns specifications, so testing can be only as good as the specification on which it is based. There are many good reasons for placing considerable emphasis on the early specification phases of a project - primarily to reduce the errors in the software - but a good specification will also produce the benefit of tests that are straightforward to plan and carry out.

In this section we outline some aspects of testing that appear repeatedly in the book: the two forms of testing (*static* and *dynamic testing*), testability, validation, and the problem of drawing up project plans that incorporate testing.

### 2.4.2    Static testing

Static tests are those that do not involve the execution of anything - be it code or executable specifications. In static testing, specifications are compared with each other to verify that errors have not been introduced during the process. Using grey arrows to denote the verification of a specification by comparing it with another, the process is illustrated in figure 2.3.

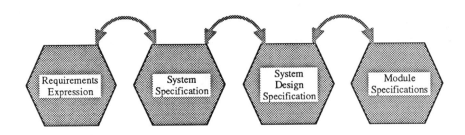

Figure 2.3 - The specifications used in static testing

Each specification phase emphasises a different aspect of software development, with each subsequent phase introducing more detail. We can express each aspect in terms of the deliverables:

- The *Requirements Expression* states what the system is expected to achieve from the end-user's point of view.
- The *System Specification* lists the functions and attributes of the actual system in detail.
- The *System Design Specification* states how the system is to be put together and, at a high level, what the overall software design of the system is to be. It includes a description of software components - subsystems or modules - and states how these components are to be structured.
- A *Module Specification* states what an item of code is expected to do and records its design. It is the basis for programming the item.

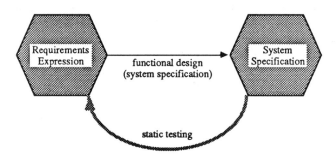

Figure 2.4 - Static testing of the System Specification

In static testing, the above documents are compared *with each other* to verify that each item accurately translates information from the previous document. For instance, figure 2.4 shows the static testing of the System Specification in terms of the life-cycle model.

In figure 2.4, the backward pointing arrow indicates that the System Specification is verified by comparing it with the Requirements Expression. Unlike the other three specifications, the Requirements Expression cannot be tested against another specification, since it is the first produced in the life-cycle.

*Consistency verification* is another form of static testing. In this form of testing, a deliverable (typically a specification) is checked to confirm that it is self-consistent; that one part of it does not contradict another. In figure 2.5 we take the example of consistency testing on the System Specification.

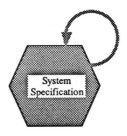

Figure 2.5 - Consistency testing on the System Specification

## 2.4.3   Dynamic testing

Dynamic testing confirms that a deliverable - typically some software - functions according to its specification. It differs from static testing in that verification is done by *executing* that deliverable rather than by comparing one specification with another. In figure 2.6 we look at the dynamic testing of the System for Trial. We can see that the System for Trial is being verified by comparing its operation with what was specified in the System Specification. The Acceptance Test Plan is the document that links the two.

*Test Plans*

In section 2.2 we identified four different types of Test Plan. The *Test Plan* is the essential link in dynamic testing. It links the specification to the item to be tested. It should include a complete description of the strategy for testing, plus test scripts and expected results. On the organisational side, it should also describe the organisation of the testing team, schedules for testing and the liaison between the team developing the software and the testing team.

Test Plans need not be produced sequentially in the life-cycle. However, a Test Plan clearly cannot be produced before the specification on which it is based, yet it must be ready in time for the dynamic testing based on it. As a general rule, it should be produced as early as possible to allow the organisation and resourcing of the tests - once more a management responsibility.

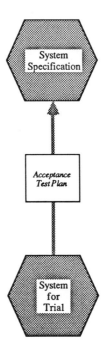

Figure 2.6 - Dynamic testing of the System for Trial

A Test Plan can be considered a translation document which links design specifications with dynamic tests. How this translation process can be verified is outlined in the following sections and covered in more detail in subsequent chapters.

The results of dynamic tests are always compared with the expected results listed in the Test Plan. Any differences can be expected to result in changes either to the design (and to any derived end products in the life-cycle) or to the tests themselves in the form of modifications to the Test Plan. After any necessary changes have been made, the tests are run again. This is illustrated in figure 2.7.

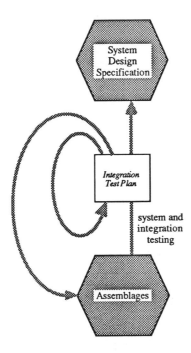

Figure 2.7 - Comparison of actual with expected test results

*Black-box and white-box testing*

Dynamic testing can be based on two different aspects of the design process. If the objective is to check whether the requirements for an object have been met, then it is called *black-box testing* - the object is treated like a black box in that inputs are pushed into it and its outputs checked against what was expected; the requirements are used as the basis for deriving the input test cases. If the testing is based on the detailed inner workings of the item, then it is *white-box testing* - the contents of the box are inspected to see how they fit together and tests are devised on the basis of that structure.

The differences between the two are illustrated in figure 2.8.

The black- and white-box views of testing together allow us to check that our dynamic testing is thorough. Between them, all aspects of the system should be covered. This can be used as a quality criterion for testing a Test Plan itself.

It is also notable that black-box testing need not only be based on the immediately preceding specification for the object being tested but may go back several steps in the design process. An example of this would be a check on a module to ensure that it implements some feature described in the System Specification.

15

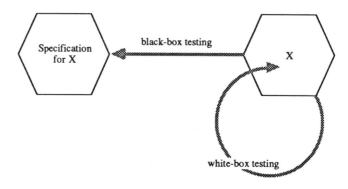

Figure 2.8 - Black-box and white-box testing

## 2.4.4    Testability

To ensure that the products of the design process are suitable for testing, it is sensible to review them for testability.   For example, if a specification is to satisfy the criterion of testability, it must be in a form suitable for translation into Test Plans. It is important that criteria for translating the specifications at various points in the life-cycle into Test Plans should be known at the time that the specifications are created.

The verification process for testability cannot be as thorough as the verifications described earlier, since the Test Plans will not have been written at the time of verification.   However, it re-emphasises the importance of knowing the material to be covered by each Test Plan.

In following chapters we look at how we can test for testability in a deliverable and suggest ways in which that testability can be ensured.   However, development is an iterative process and specifications and other deliverables are often worked and reworked many times. As a consequence, in common with everything else, their entropy increases and they become ever more "untidy".   A direct result is that a design or whatever can become increasingly more difficult to test and this degeneration of the testability of something is a symptom of its general degeneration - something that requires detection and action by management.   Some ways in which the testability of a deliverable - a design, a source module or whatever - can be destroyed during development are listed in the following table:

*How the testability of a deliverable can degenerate*

Amendments (whether repairs, additions or deletions) that are not controlled lead to a weakened and/or complicated deliverable.

Constructs in the languages or methods being used that do not fit well with the nature of the function being provided lead to circumlocutions and thence to errors.

Conflict between a deliverable and its documentation results from changes made without sufficient care and control.

Accidents, misunderstandings and the gradual substitution of one person's perceptions and assumptions for those of the originator of the deliverable result in distortions to the design.

Insufficient time, training or resources lead to deviations from the design.

Insufficient resources and low priority lead to incomplete or shallow testing.

Unavailability of supporting tools and functions of sufficient quality leads to inconclusive or inaccurate testing.

Poor control of testing leads to items being insufficiently tested, not tested at all, or not reported as being tested.

An inadequate theory and practice of testing leads to work that cannot be objectively measured or judged.

## 2.4.5   Verification and validation

Two terms frequently come across in the testing literature are *validation* and *verification*. Many different definitions can be found but we use some that have widespread currency. Verification is the testing of an object against its specification. Validation is the process of confirming that a deliverable matches the user's expectations (probably recorded in the Requirements Expression).

Thus we talk about verifying module source code against the module's specification and about verifying a Module Specification against the System Design Specification.

We also talk about validating any specification or other deliverable against the Requirements Expression. However, it is unusual to base any *formal* testing on the Requirements Expression. This is due to the difficulty of producing specific tests of what are often imprecise user expectations about how the system should perform. Instead, the final group of validation tests that we address in this book are the Acceptance Tests, which are based on the more precise System Specification.

The validation of the delivered system is often the subject of a legal agreement between the supplier of the software and the client and it can take many forms. In many cases, the client approves the System Specification and then the successful completion of Acceptance Testing will act as validation of the system. In other cases, the system is expected to perform without "problems" after it is put into service: in this case the warranty and post-delivery periods constitute validation of the system.

Two common methods for easing the difficulties of validation are *prototyping* and *animation*. In prototyping, a part or early version of the system is implemented in some fashion so that users can observe it in practice. Through an iterative process, the Requirements Expression can be refined into a document that more precisely defines user expectations. Animations are similar to prototypes but do not necessarily involve the development of a computer system to demonstrate operation to the user. Two methods currently used (albeit somewhat experimentally) are the preparation of the System Specification in a formal language which can be translated automatically into a system suitable for inspection by the user, and the preparation of examples based on the Requirements Expression or System Specification which users can inspect for correctness and agreement with their expectations. We take up these issues in chapter 3.

In the terminology of this book, prototyping and animation are *static* validation, in that they are tests on the specifications for the system. A *dynamic* form of validation is the *pilot system*. Here a live system is produced, although with only a selection of the features to be provided by the full system. It might be installed on one or more pilot sites. The users then try out the pilot system and judge whether it meets their needs. Using this feedback, the requirements for the full system are refined and ultimately validated. Depending on the development philosophy for the project, the pilot can be expanded into the full system, or the full system can be written from scratch.

## 2.4.6    Translating the life-cycle diagram into a project plan

It is important to be pragmatic in setting the level of testing to be undertaken on a given project. There is a cost attached to not testing but there will be a high development cost attached to very thorough testing. So managers must make a trade-off between the time spent on testing activities and the risk of failure following delivery. This trade-off is made visible by the way that the life-cycle is turned into a project plan. Some testing activities will appear; others will be omitted.

The sections above discuss the wide variety of tests that are relevant to software development. Although they are useful for specific needs on a software project, not all forms of testing are always required and the ones that are used should depend on what the system is expected to do and how it is put together. For example, for critical components of a system it is essential that testing be very thorough and

18

cover all the forms discussed above. It is especially important to do thorough white-box testing and rigorous integration tests to confirm that system components are properly integrated and do not produce undesirable side effects. Static verification of design specifications is essential for such applications and has led to considerable research into formal specification methods that allow proofs of correctness and the automated verification of specifications.

Applications that are less critical will not require all the forms of testing. For example, if there are few interfaces or side effects between units of code, it is feasible to drop the integration step from the life-cycle. If the functionality of the system maps closely onto the program structure and there is little risk of internal side effects, then we may not need to do white-box testing except at the unit code level.

In terms of the timing of activities in the generic life-cycle model, a number of activities can be performed in parallel. In particular, static testing of a specification and preparation of the Test Plan based on that specification can be done simultaneously. This can be helped by a project team structure that uses different people for static testing and dynamic testing, since the latter would normally prepare the Test Plans.

## 2.5     Change management

### 2.5.1    Configuration management

*Configuration management* is the complete mechanism for controlling and recording the status of all deliverables, their relationships and their changes. It allows the manager to determine the state of software development at all times. Testing is dependent on good configuration management, since testing is the constant checking of one developed item against another, as we can see from the life-cycle model. Since those items are in a state of constant change, the process of comparison can be controlled only if the status of each item is known at all times. In practice, it is impossible to test any reasonably sized system without a good system of configuration management in place.

In section 2.4 we saw that specifications are the basis for all testing. Consequently, it is essential that specifications are subject to the same configuration management controls as software items.

Configuration management is a large subject with a literature of its own, eg [Bersoff 1981], but there are three aspects that concern testing:

- change control
- version control
- record keeping.

We now take these in turn.

## 2.5.2   Change control

Software development is a process of change. But by its nature testing creates fixed points - tested specifications, tested code and so on. So it becomes vital to control all changes to items relevant to tests. When we change a deliverable we can read off the actions we must take from the life-cycle diagram. In particular, three key areas are:

- the need to keep Test Plans up to date when designs and other deliverables change
- the need to modify code, specifications, user documentation and dynamic tests when errors are revealed by testing
- the need to retest items whose specifications have changed.

For instance, suppose that the system design is changed. This will be reflected by changes in the System Design Specification, and possibly by changes later in the life-cycle to module design and coding. For *static* testing, specifications documenting those later phases must be verified to confirm that they reflect the change to the design. For *dynamic* testing, the Integration Test Plan, as well as the tests it incorporates, must also be modified to reflect the changes in the System Design Specification. If there are any changes to later design phases, later testing specifications also have to be modified.

The change control process is similar if we discover errors from testing. When the presence of an error is suggested by a test, we need to check whether the error is "genuine" - ie in the object being tested - in which case some deliverables in the life-cycle will require modification. For errors found in static testing, it is generally the design document(s) that will require revision; for errors found in dynamic testing, either the item being tested or the specification on which the test is based or both item and specification will require modification. If the error is in the test itself, the test is modified and the change recorded in the change control records.

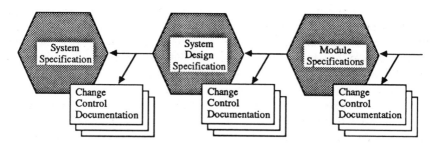

Figure 2.9 - Changes cascading back through deliverables

20

In addition to the items directly affected by the change, there is often a "cascade" effect on other end products in the life-cycle. For design errors, specifications prior to the item in question must also be changed if the errors found are reflected there. Figure 2.9 illustrates how a fault discovered in a module during module testing can mean changes to its Module Specification and in turn to the System Design Specification.

## 2.5.3    Version control

During system development and subsequent maintenance, most deliverables will be worked on iteratively and thus go through several versions. This may occur simultaneously for different deliverables in the life-cycle. Testing cannot be done sensibly unless the version of each item relevant to the test is known and confirmed as the *correct* version for the test. This applies to the items on which the test is based as well as the items being tested.

This form of control is especially important when subsystems or entire systems are being built and then tested. Each version of the built item will contain a particular version of each of its components, and the management of this process requires thorough record-keeping of those versions. If the testing team is separate from the design and development team(s), then it is crucial to establish a close but formal liaison between them to coordinate the versions of items being tested, as well as the tests themselves.

## 2.5.4    Record-keeping and traceability

Neither change nor version control can function without adequate record-keeping. Yet it is not a simple matter to determine the best record-keeping system for a software project - in other words, one that keeps adequate records without being cumbersome or time-consuming.

In this situation, the best criterion is that of *traceability*, the ability to establish an *audit trail* of relevant information. In the context of testing, this can be interpreted as the ability to trace an error to its source. This is *not* a trivial problem when that source may lie several design steps before the step currently under test. To provide for traceability, each item in the chain should provide full cross-referencing of its components to the item on which it is based. For example, each component in the System Design Specification should be cross-referenced as far as possible to those features in the System Specification that it implements.

Another aspect of traceability in testing is the ability to follow the progress of errors revealed by testing. For each error found, it should be possible to trace the process of correction through the audit trail from the point where the error was found to the point where it was corrected.

A final criterion of traceability is the ability to trace the static and dynamic tests that were performed on an item after each change in its development history. This implies that the record-keeping system should allow you to obtain a full history of all items - software, documentation and tests - that are part of the development process. Such records have added value in that they can yield data on the testing itself, thereby helping the project to improve the quality of its product. A scan of test histories at the end of a project can often be useful to subsequent projects by highlighting problem areas and approaches that proved effective.

## 2.6    Special management concerns in testing

### 2.6.1    Educating staff

Testing is just as creative and intellectual as system design or program design, the creativity being in writing test scripts, and the intellectual effort in trying to break the system and to prove that it is imperfect. A good test run is one that does not work!

The frustration of testing experienced by many software engineers - especially programmers when testing their programs - stems from the wish to prove that the system is *correct* - the opposite of what is really called for. Staff have to accept that their role is to try and find faults and finally reach the point where they cannot find any more faults - even though some might still exist. Only through testing can it be ensured that the resulting deliverable is the one that works for the user in the user's environment and not one that is technically interesting but out of tune with the user's true needs.

Staff need to be trained in techniques for testing in the same way that they are taught programming languages, database design and other technical areas of software engineering. Training must be given to everyone - including the users. It is especially important that users are trained to test the systems that they are to approve and accept.

As with any project activity, testing must be correctly managed:

- clear responsibility must be assigned
- clear authority must be given
- budgets should be based on the cost of system failure due to inadequate testing
- suitable resources and skills must be assigned
- essential skills must be provided through training
- appropriate tools must be bought or built
- an adequate amount of time should be budgetted.

## 2.6.2    Contractual requirements and testing objectives

Managers must ensure that before any testing the objectives of that testing are known and agreed and that the objectives are set in terms that can be measured. Test objectives need to be set at each stage of the development life-cycle and should be quantified, reasonable and achievable.  It is especially important that results are measurable: for example, it may be a requirement that all tests be passed under a certain set of conditions, such as predefined load on the system.

It is especially important that managers recognise the contractual requirements.  Managers are effectively contracted to produce an acceptable and tested product.  This "contractual" requirement may even have to stand the test of litigation, so the organisation must be set up to record objectives and whether those objectives are met, as demonstrated by suitable testing.

## 2.6.3    Establishing a budget for testing

Testing must be cost-effective and tied to the cost of production and the cost of failure.  The budget for testing can be viewed as a form of insurance whose premium reflects its necessity and the cost of failure.

Managers should quantify testing activity to the extent that a certain level of testing will cost a certain amount of time and/or money.  This level of testing, like insurance, will cover categories of possible failure.  The budget will cover all forms of prototyping, reviews and walkthroughs as well as code testing, system testing and so on.

Clearly some development projects will require very little testing (insurance) while others could require enormous budgets.  One-off, non-critical reports will attract a low budget for testing expressed as a proportion of the development effort, whereas real-time aircraft control systems will attract a much larger budget.  However, if the one-off report is to be used as the basis for a huge investment, then the budget for testing the accuracy of that report should be much larger.  There is no "standard level" of testing that should be applied whatever the object being tested.

This makes the setting of testing budgets a difficult matter but a rule of thumb is to ensure that the budget for both time and resources is about 40% of the overall project budget.  Within the industry a wide variation has been quoted: some simple jobs might have a zero budget, whilst testing for highly critical systems might take 80% of the development cost.  Only by keeping records of the amount of time actually spent on each testing activity *and of the effectiveness of that testing* can managers start to build up a profile of the budget requirements for testing in the application areas in which they work, the organisation they work for, and the types of system they build.

## 2.6.4    Planning the tests

The following aspects should be considered for every test:

* test philosophy and criticality
* objectives and completion criteria
* methods
* responsibilities and people involved
* resources and test tools
* budget
* schedule
* documentation
* problem recording
* problem fixing.

The tests must be organised, which means determining:

* their sequence and timing
* the people involved and when
* the implications for other systems being developed or run
* an estimate of the time required
* the deliverable items
* that resources will be available when needed.

The documentation involved is as extensive as that of the very production process that is being tested.  Typical documents are:

* a Test Management Plan, for instance as a hierarchical set of bar-charts identifying critical points and dependencies
* advice of the test to those involved
* Test Plans describing inputs, expected actual output, objectives
* Test Log.

After tests are completed, both the Test Plan and test results should be archived for the life of the system.  Later they will be useful for maintenance or possible extensions to the system and pehaps in future projects.  In extreme cases, test results might be used to defend the producers against litigation.  There is increasing pressure on software developers to take the same level of responsibility for the effects of using their software as is expected of the makers of children's toys, automobiles and nuclear power reactors.  Governmental and international legislation will increasingly demand that they are using the best methods possible and consequently they will need to be able to prove that they are doing so.

## 2.6.5    Establishing a method

There are many methods for testing - the rest of this book describes some of the testing methods available. Managers need to establish a formal and appropriate process for testing. It is not enough to set up a standards manual and expect people to follow it: the method of testing needs to be taught along with the skills required to judge the suitability of a particular technique.

The system development team will need clear management support in establishing a range of methods. The management action should be to remove dogma and the blind application of a limited set of standards and instead to select and apply techniques suitable to the project in hand.

The maintenance of records to establish the success or failure of individual techniques is important. Other areas of engineering have successfully established techniques such as Quality Circles. It is up to software development managers to establish similar Quality Circles within software development teams.

## 2.6.6    Starting early

The later an error is detected, the more it costs to correct. This cost includes the "landslide" cost to items later in the life-cycle, and will generally be made worse by the fact that the further from its source an error is found, the harder it is to trace the source. Moreover, an increasing number of people are involved in error detection and correction in the later stages of the life-cycle and program code that has been corrected or otherwise modified is more likely to contain errors because of unexpected side-effects. In the following table we list some key points about starting early on testing and test planning.

*Starting early on testing*

It is never too early to start testing.
Early testing means starting with the Requirements Expression.
Early testing starts with the establishment of a plan.
Early testing starts with the establishment of a management team which may include:
- management
- users
- business analysts
- technical analysts
- operations analysts
- auditors.

The team will need additional technical skills from all areas:
- user
- technical
- operations
- auditing.

The longer that defects are left in the system the more it costs to put the system right.

## 2.6.7    Testing through the life of the system

Once a system is installed it will need to be kept running. Software does not wear out like machinery but it becomes unsuitable because of a large number of factors. Among them are:

- growth
- environmental changes
- changes in requirements
- legislation changes
- hardware and other technology changes
- changes in the economics of alternatives.

The system will need continued testing to establish how well it fits the requirements. As with all testing there is a completion criterion and with this sort of testing there is the additional need for a criterion to determine when and how much testing is required.

## 2.6.8    Measurement and data collection

Improvements in the effectiveness of testing can come only through experience, and so it is important to extract data from the development and testing process. This data is generally kept by individual software developers, but a national databank for the UK has been established (1985) by the Alvey Directorate in the form of the *Software Data Library*. It is expected that contributors will supply data to the library, which can then be accessed by individual users for information on the effectiveness of development and testing methods.

The sort of data you can collect and analyse yourself is listed in the following table.

*Data to be collected during development for each error found*

A short narrative description of the symptoms and the cause.
The severity of the error, perhaps along the following lines:
- major architectural changes required
- minor architectural changes required
- small changes required in several places
- changes of detail required in one place
- documentation change only.

A classification of the cause, classified perhaps along the following lines:
- error in the use of proprietary software (such as a DBMS)
- error in the use of an internal software interface
- error in the use of an interface with a piece of hardware
- function not implemented
- etc.

The stage of development at which the error was made.
The stage of development at which the error was detected.
The effort required to clear the error.
The possible cost had the error remained undetected.
Actions that would have led to the earlier detection of the error.

Collecting this data for errors detected during dynamic testing, ie from Unit Testing onwards, is relatively straightforward although it can be time-consuming without automated support for collection and analysis. Collecting it during the earlier specification phases is more difficult and requires more discipline.

If you keep such records yourself they can help you in the following ways:

- *Am I always making the same sort of mistakes in the same areas?* Records will indicate whether there are constant sources of errors affecting the quality of particular end products.
- *How effective are my testing procedures?* Analysis of the records may show that the testing itself, rather than the items tested, tends to be at fault. This can lead you to a more effective testing practices.
- *How do I know when to stop testing?* As a rule, the rate of discovering errors decreases as bugs are fixed (although the rate can increase at the start of testing if a large number of corrections introduce new errors into the system). By measuring the error rates and classifying the errors found, projects are given a rational criterion to use for declaring the completion of testing.

# Chapter 3 - The User's View of Testing

## 3.1    Introduction

This chapter concentrates on testing in those parts of the development life-cycle that directly concern the intended user of a system. Figure 3.1 shows the relevant fragment of the development model and we can see from it that we are concerned with the following products:

* the *Requirements Expression*
* the *System Specification*
* the *System for Trial*
* the *Delivered System.*

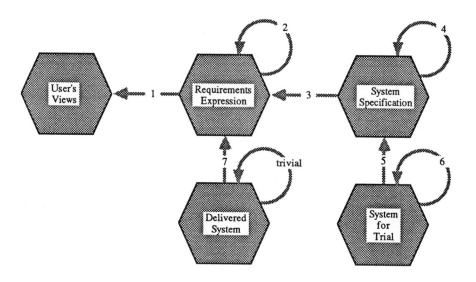

Figure 3.1 - The user's view of testing during the life-cycle

It is worthwhile being clear what these objects are, so the following paragraphs characterise them in a way appropriate to their meaning in this book - different organisations use different terms with different meanings and you will need to map our terms onto those that you use in your own organisation.

The *Requirements Expression* describes what the user wants to achieve with a system. It can involve organisational, financial, or technical matters. It might say "any system that we buy must generate benefits X, Y, and Z". It might say "we actually need a system that does this or that because they are the benefits we want or because they are needed if we are to get the benefits we want". In other words it might express a very high level desire or a quite specific feature. The key point is that the Requirements Expression describes aims and specifies a class of systems.

The *System Specification* describes a system that would satisfy the requirements stated in the Requirements Expression. The description is detailed because it is the basis of design. The key point is that the System Specification describes one system satisfying the Requirements Expression and specifies a class of possible implementations. (It is worth noting in passing that the System Design Specification describes one of the class of possible implementations satisfying the System Specification.)

The *System for Trial* is a system that has been prepared to satisfy the System Specification. It is one *implementation* of the System Specification.

The *Delivered System* is the system that emerges from the development process and is used by the intended user. It should satisfy the requirements expressed in the Requirements Expression.

So, now that we have identified the objects that concern the user, what tests can we identify that involve these objects? There are seven that we can read off from the life-cycle model fragment and we can divide them into three sets. (The numbering refers to the numbering on the arrows in figure 3.1.)

The first set of tests centres on the Requirements Expression and the Delivered System:

- testing that the Requirements Expression is a complete and correct expression of the user's requirements (1)
- testing that the Requirements Expression is internally consistent and has "desirable" properties (2).

The second set of tests is grouped around the System Specification:

- testing that the System Specification describes a system that will satisfy the user's requirements as expressed in the Requirements Expression (3)
- testing that the System Specification is "in itself " correct and has "desirable" properties (4).

The third set centres on the System for Trial and the Delivered System:

- testing that the System for Trial is a correct implementation of the System Specification using the Acceptance Test Plan (5)
- testing that the System for Trial is correct in itself (6)
- testing that the Delivered System lives up to the expectations originally set down in the Requirements Expression (7).

The last of these - the testing of the Delivered System against the Requirements Expression (and indeed the User's Views) - is something outside the scope of this book. It relates to the continuing process of change that occurs to a system once it has gone into service, as it reveals its characteristics in use and as user requirements themselves change. We therefore do not cover this further.

The rest of this chapter is divided into three sections that deal with each set of tests in turn. Section 3.2 describes the Requirements Expression and its relationship to the user; section 3.3 describes the System Specification and its relationship to the user and to the Requirements Expression; and section 3.4 describes the System for Trial and its relationship to the System Specification.

## 3.2    Testing the Requirements Expression

### 3.2.1    Introduction

The development of any new system, like that of a building, requires firm foundations. If a building's foundations are weak or faulty then the likelihood is that it will eventually collapse. So it is with software systems.

The foundations on which a system is built are the user's requirements. These requirements need to be expressed as correctly as possible to avoid any failings in the system that is to be produced. The analysis of the requirements is therefore of paramount importance to the later phases of development.

Missing, inflexible, misunderstood, and ambiguously or incorrectly expressed requirements can all result in problems. How do they arise in the first place? The Requirements Expression will be based on discussions between analysts and the eventual users of the system, and on investigation as to how any current system works - many users will not have dealt with computer analysts before, might not realise what information is required of them and might even be openly hostile to the introduction of a new system and to changes in their working practices. Despite this difficulty, the Requirements Expression must be produced successfully if the system is to be built. What information is required to fulfil this role and how can we test the requirements produced? That is what this section covers.

The first thing we must do is define what a *requirement* is. In this book we define it as *a condition or capability needed by a user to solve a problem or achieve an objective*. So, a requirement does not involve any design work, but is just a consequence of the business (or any other) needs of the user.

The Requirements Expression will be a description of the environment in which the system will work, plus a list of requirements that the system will have to fulfil. The total list of requirements must provide a firm and internally consistent basis for the specification and design of the future system.

The only way of establishing the requirements for the system is to interview interested parties: those who will actually use the system, those who will pay for it, those who will audit it, those who will be concerned for its security and the security of the information held on it, those concerned with the reliability and safety of the system, and many more. In what follows we will refer to them collectively as the *user* or *customer*.

Good communication between the analysts and the user is of major importance and, since it is the only way of establishing requirements, the user must be able to understand the final output from this phase of development - the Requirements Expression. The Requirements Expression needs to be intelligible to the user, stating clearly what the requirements are as defined by the analyst. It should be the analyst's job to decide how to test the statement of requirements but the user is the final arbiter on the correctness of the Requirements Expression.

One of the major problems in system design is the cost of wrong or missing statements of requirements. If a requirement is wrongly expressed, and this is not detected, then the error will infiltrate later phases of development, with the cost of repair increasing the longer the error remains undetected. A Requirements Expression therefore has to be tested thoroughly to ensure that the requirements are correct. Yet requirements, because of their nature, are not easy to identify, and checking that all requirements have been covered is even more awkward.

In the following sections we look at the criteria we should expect a Requirements Expression to satisfy if it is to be a successful foundation and then we look at some of the methods we can use to check a Requirements Expression against them.

## 3.2.2   Criteria for testing a Requirements Expression

The testing criteria used at this stage are intended to prove that the Requirements Expression covers as many requirements as are realistically within the scope of the system. We look at *completeness, consistency, feasibility, testability*, and *referability*.

*Completeness*

Once a project has been agreed its scope must be clearly defined. Without such a framework it is easy for the requirements to expand continually to cover areas that the users feel could be covered. Ensuring that all of the customer's requirements are included might at first seem a laudable aim, but it could mean we never progress beyond the requirements phase as the system's scope increases indefinitely.

The first test of a Requirements Expression is therefore: "has the system's scope been clearly delimited?". Without a clear statement of scope it becomes difficult to decide whether the Requirements Expression is complete and at the same time difficult to stop it growing endlessly.

Once the scope has been established, obvious gaps can be looked for. The first thing to ensure is that all users of the data to be handled by the system have been contacted. This includes "owners" of data as well as those who originate the data, those who input it and those who receive reports, summaries and any other data deriving from the system. Where there is an existing or related system (perhaps manual) it will be possible to interview its users. Where a new system is being developed its prospective users need to be identified.

Each of the users in this group of interested parties should be given a list, in an understandable form, of the requirements so far identified so that they can check for omissions and errors. The aim is to establish that, for all the users, all of the requirements have been identified. This list should also be shown to management, auditors and those paying the bill.

The ensuing discussions will help the analyst to check for the completeness of the Requirements Expression. It will often be necessary to reconcile users' perceived requirements for the system with its defined scope, and in some instances to refer irreconcilable differences to the person on the users' side who has the authority to adjudicate on what goes in and what stays out.

Once an agreed set of requirements has been compiled in the Requirements Expression there are some simple checks for completeness:

- Are there any unfinished statements? For instance, "the system should be able to support ?? users", "the query language for the order processing facility should be compatible with ??". Besides being obviously incomplete, such statements often hide areas that could not be agreed on or were so difficult to solve they were left unresolved!

- Are there references to non-existent objects? "The system should provide configuration management and control as specified in the British Standard" (yes, but which?). "In cases of missing personnel records the system should inform the user as previously explained" (where?). "The satellite radio boom should be activated as explained in section 3.2.1" (which doesn't exist). Check all references explicit and implicit to ensure that the object referred to actually exists and is relevant.

- Have all system attributes been covered as well as all of its functionality? For instance,
  - back-up or recovery facilities required
  - future interfacing requirements
  - diagnostic levels to be supported
  - the domain of use ("between 20°N and 20°S", "between -20°C and +40°C", etc)
  - performance and throughput
  - reliability, maintainability, portability, and all the other -abilities that describe some property of the system
  - documentation to be supplied
  - the resources that can be assumed for its operation
  - the resources that can be assumed for its development
  - and so on.
- Areas of omission are obviously difficult to spot, but discussion with each user looking at it from their particular viewpoint and consideration of exactly what they expect the system to do should help to point out many of these omissions.

---

*Checking for completeness*

Do all the requirements fit into a well-defined framework?

Is the system's scope well-defined?

Are there any obvious omissions?

Have all the users of the system been identified?

Are there any unfinished statements in the Requirements Expression?

Are there any references to things that do not exist or are irrelevant?

Are there any general areas omitted?

Are all the requirements explicitly stated?

---

*Consistency*

Having established the requirements for an area we now need to check whether any of them contradict each other. Contradictions and inconsistencies both lead to problems in later phases of system development as they will be interpreted differently by different people. They need to be checked for and removed as soon as possible. This might mean bringing users together to discuss the problem and to identify a consistent and mutually agreeable set of requirements.

Successful checking for consistency demands that the requirements are understood by all who read them. If a requirement is full of jargon, especially computer jargon, how can the user understand it? All requirements should be kept as free of jargon as possible, enabling users, computer professionals and auditors to understand what is going on. If jargon has to be used then the Requirements Expression should contain a glossary so that anyone coming across an expression for the first time can interpret it correctly.

The sort of *internal inconsistency* to be checked for is the following: "... the system shall react to inputs from external lines at all times with a maximum response time of 30 seconds ... the system shall provide interactive processing each day between 0700 hours and 2000 hours only". The first statement can be read to mean that the system is available for input round the clock, in contradiction to the second statement.

The Requirements Expression must also be checked for *external inconsistency*. External documents referred to from the Requirements Expression have to be checked to ensure that they are consistent with the Requirements Expression. For instance, our Requirements Expression might require that "the system will use the existing PC4 process control system and will serve up to 40 control points", whilst the specification for the PC4 system might say "the PC4 system provides support for at most 15 control points".

Even more difficult to spot is the *circular inconsistency*. This is where three or more statements in the Requirements Expression (or, worse still, the Requirements Expression and other documents) form a contradiction when taken together. These can be very difficult to spot and require great awareness on the part of the author and reviewers of the Requirements Expression, including the users.

Finally, consistency in the use of terms must be checked for. Synonyms and homonyms should be avoided. Experience shows that the process of spelling out the meaning of terms in great detail itself frequently reveals misunderstandings and errors in a Requirements Expression. A simple glossary can assist.

---

*Checking for consistency*

Are there any contradictions?
Are the requirements understandable to the user?
Are the requirements free of jargon?
Are there external inconsistencies?
Are there internal inconsistencies?
Are there any circular inconsistencies?
Are there unnecessary synonyms?
Are there unnecessary homonyms?

---

Ensuring that the Requirements Expression is consistent is the analyst's job, but it can only be done with user agreement at all stages of the project. If the finished Requirements Expression is incomprehensible to the users then they cannot review it or agree with it.

### Feasibility

If a requirement is infeasible then there is no point in specifying it. A requirement such as "any subsequent change in user requirements should be implementable within one day" is clearly impractical, but infeasibility can be quite subtle and even simple-sounding requirements can prove technically difficult or expensive to implement. "All screen transactions must be recorded simultaneously on hard copy" sounds innocent enough but could prove infeasible if screen transactions involve the use of graphics or input via mouse, touchscreen, joystick, or voice.

---

### Checking for feasibility

> Is the requirement practicable?
> Can the requirement be incorporated alongside other requirements?
> Does the requirement preclude desirable growth paths?
> Is the requirement cost-effective?
> Would a system with the required feature be maintainable cost-effectively?
> Is the requirement justified?

---

Whenever a user specifies a requirement it should be investigated in detail. Will it be possible to incorporate it alongside the other requirements so far identified? Is the technology up to the requirement (especially in the case of performance or reliability requirements)? Does the requirement preclude growth paths which might be required in the life of the system? Answering these questions often means doing some basic investigations into available technologies or even designs.

The requirements must also be cost-effective. There is no point in having a requirement that seems reasonable to the user if the cost of implementing it plus the cost of maintaining and running it is outside the available resources or exceeds the value of the likely benefits. It might be necessary to trim the requirements on the system to fit the resources available and quantification of costs and benefits can be difficult. Gilb's *Design by Objectives* [Gilb 1986], for instance, gives the system-builder techniques for handling this situation.

*Design by Objectives* uses a hierarchical decomposition technique to break vague statements about system attributes down into smaller, quantified statements that identify worst acceptable, best imaginable and likely levels. For example, the notion of *robustness* is a vague one but we can decompose it into more precise, *quantified* notions by specifying for instance how the system will behave if its mains supply is cut off and restored or if 20% of its incoming messages have a single parity error and 3% have two parity errors.

### *Testability*

What do we mean by a *testable requirement*? A Requirements Expression states what the users expect from the system. The final system should fulfil that expectation, so it becomes crucial for us to be able to take a system intended to satisfy a Requirements Expression and check whether it does. Therefore a Requirements Expression is *testable* if we can carry out this check on the implemented system. We cannot leave this check for testability until the system has been built; we must assess the Requirements Expression when it is written.

How can we get a testable Requirements Expression to start with? The only way is to quantify requirements as far as possible. If the requirement is quantified then there is a definite point at which the user can say that it has (or has not) been met. Even if the requirement cannot be precisely quantified then the analyst should at least try to ensure that as much quantification as possible (in terms of permissible ranges and so on) is included. Look for ways of increasing the quantification of each requirement - *Design by Objectives* can help here again.

In particular, avoid statements like "the software shall provide real-time response", or "the software shall be easy to use". Neither of these could be checked for in a system. But a statement such as "the system must provide sufficient on-line help and guidance to allow a novice user to perform all of the transactions A through to H listed above without resort to a manual" could reasonably be tested for. Although it is not numerically quantified it would be possible for the users to test the requirement by getting a novice user to try to use the system. If they can use all those transactions with the aid of the help facilities then the requirement has been met.

Any requirement that is specified must be understandable to the users but it must also be specific and unambiguous. If a statement of requirement is not specific or contains ambiguities then whenever people come to use that statement as a basis for definition or design they may make different interpretations of the requirement and these might consequently give rise to a system failure. The more specific the statement the easier the requirement will be to test and the simpler it should be to agree. Complex statements of requirement can easily lead to misinterpretation and consequently errors. One of the basic maxims of all systems work applies as much here as to implementation: *keep it simple*.

*Checking for testability*

> Is each requirement understandable by the users?
> Is each requirement specific?
> Is each requirement unambiguous?
> Is each requirement quantified?
> Could you test for the requirement in an implemented system?

*Referability*

Each requirement must be labelled in some form to allow ease of reference in related documents such as the System Specification. Discussions about the requirements in later stages can get very confusing, especially if there are a number of similar ones. Problems of interpretation can be alleviated if it is possible to identify exactly which requirement a subsequent design decision is related to. A requirements list can then be very useful in checking that all requirements have been carried on into subsequent stages.

So one test to be carried out on the Requirements Expression is this: *is every statement of requirement uniquely identifiable?*

## 3.2.3 Techniques for testing a Requirements Expression

There are a number of techniques that can be used to test whether the Requirements Expression satisfies the criteria we have discussed above. Any one technique will generally not be enough, so a combination of them is generally used to ensure that all of the criteria are covered. Our assumption here is that the Requirements Expression is probably written in English and, to that extent, is informally expressed (as opposed to some of the formal means of expression that we can use on the System Specification, for example). Our checking methods will therefore be equally informal (in the mathematical sense) though we can expect them to be thorough.

*Reading and checking*

Giving users the Requirements Expression to read allows them to highlight requirements that are wrong from their viewpoint, areas in the Requirements Expression that conflict with each other (internal inconsistencies) and areas that are difficult to understand. However, reading the Requirements Expression on its own will not cause all the errors to be found and so reading is generally used as essential preparation for interviews and formal reviews of the sort discussed below. If the reading is not to be undirected, an essential input to simple reading is checklists of the type also described below.

*Interviews*

An *interview* is based on relatively informal communications between two people - the analyst and the user. There are two types of interview to be considered here.

The first is the direct person-to-person interview. In this case the analyst talks directly to the user with the aim of identifying errors in the Requirements Expression. The user should be interviewed only about the areas and interfaces that they are involved with. The analyst's job is to act as Devil's advocate. (If anyone were to attempt to *prove* the Requirements Expression they would almost certainly succeed! If they attempt to pull it apart they are more likely to find the errors.)

The second type of interview is where the analyst "animates" the Requirements Expression. It is then up to the user to describe the sort of situations or input data that they would expect the system to deal with. Again the user must be encouraged to find fault with the system by checking both normal and strange situations. The analyst examines the Requirements Expression to determine what the system would do in the hypothesised situation. If the system's specified reaction matches the expectation of the user then all is well. If not then the difference has to be resolved by the analyst and the Requirements Expression correspondingly revised.

*Reviews*

One of the best ways to test a Requirements Expression is to hold a *review*. During a review, a group of people critically examine the document to check its acceptability.

A review needs to be properly organised to be effective and the first thing to do is to decide who should be present. Typically one would expect to see a user representative or representatives, the person responsible for the production of the Requirements Expression, and the person who will take the Requirements Expression through the next phase of development - system specification. Others who might be interested include auditors, those who will take over the system's maintenance and the Quality Assurance department . The review chairperson (or *moderator*) should be a representative of the manager of the user area that requires the system. As the system is to be owned by them it is up to them to ensure that the Requirements Expression fulfils expectations. All attenders must prepare by reading the material to be reviewed.

In a review of the sort described by Yourdon's *Structured Walkthroughs* [Yourdon 1979], the author of the Requirements Expression presents each statement in the Requirements Expression in turn and the other attenders critically examine it against the criteria we have discussed above. Reviewers restrict themselves to detecting errors in the Requirements Expression without attempting to correct them. This is left to its author after the review. However, if the Requirements Expression is small or only a subset of it is being reviewed it is possible for the reviewers to look for and agree on a solution to each fault found, but this can result in long arguments unless the review is strongly chaired. The aim is always to get the Requirements Expression to a point at which it can be agreed by those who have a say in it. At the end of the review the reviewers decide whether, once the identified errors have been corrected, the Requirements Expression should be re-reviewed before it is agreed and accepted by the parties concerned.

Other review techniques are available and will be found described in the literature: [Fagan 1976] covers *Fagan Inspections* which are designed principally for design and code reviewing but can be extended to requirements, and [Freedman 1979] gives many checklists and procedures especially relevant to requirements.

*Checklists*

Checklists can be very useful in determining what has been missed from the Requirements Expression and for checking what is there, but they should not be taken as the only way of testing a Requirements Expression since a checklist cannot determine the correctness of a Requirements Expression.

The following checklist can be applied to each individual statement in the Requirements Expression:

---

*Checks for individual Requirements Expression statements*

Is the requirement specific?
Is the requirement unambiguous?
Is the requirement testable in the delivered system?
Is the requirement achievable?
Is the requirement necessary?
Is the requirement maintainable?
Are types of user associated with particular requirements?
Have the users agreed to the requirement?
Is the requirement recorded in a form acceptable to both users and developers?

If a requirement gives a benefit to the purchasing organisation, is that benefit recorded and quantified?
If not, are the reasons for having the requirement recorded and agreed?
Is every statement uniquely identifiable?

The next checklist can be used to check the Requirements Expression as a whole:

*Checklist for the entire Requirements Expression*

Are the requirements complete?
Are inter-relationships between the individual requirements identified?
Have future requirements been considered?
Has everyone who will be affected by the system been consulted and have they agreed?
Do the requirements form a consistent whole?
Are there any gaps in the Requirements Expression?
Is the total package achievable?

Any organisation should refine these checklists for its own use and use them in preparation for reviews and interviews and in the reviews themselves. In particular, such organisation-specific checklists will cover questions that are relevant to the business area of the organisation and to the types of software used. In the financial software area, the security of data and auditing requirements can be expected to feature in the Requirements Expression, whilst in a safety-critical application area requirements might be placed on levels of reliability, on fall-back capability and so on.

The resulting checklists will be particularly important to the analyst who will want to draw up a very specific checklist for the system being analysed. Past experience must be used to make the checklist thorough. This will include using experience both of the application area concerned and of building similar systems. However, it must be remembered that the *correctness* of the Requirements Expression can, in the event, only be established by the user.

Organisations should also refine their checklists so that they are relevant to their own quality standards and methods of working.

## 3.3    Testing the System Specification

### 3.3.1    Introduction

The System Specification describes in detail precisely what a system is to do and holds a key position in the relationship between customer and supplier. It is very often the *contractual* definition of the system that the supplier has undertaken to supply to the customer. Any "failure" in the System Specification can mean a failure in the project - a technical failure or a commercial failure or both. So for a project to be successful both technically and commercially the quality of the System Specification is of crucial importance and must therefore be tested at the outset - at the time it is produced.

In this section we look at what is meant by "testing a System Specification" and then discuss in detail the various aspects of such testing.

### 3.3.2    How does one test a System Specification?

"Testing a System Specification" means two complementary things:

- *Qualification*: does this specification itself have desirable qualities or properties, eg consistency, unambiguity and testability?
- *Validation*: does this specification describe a system which will satisfy the user's requirements? This has two aspects:
    - does it describe a system with desirable properties, eg one that is fail-safe, is of a certain maximum size, runs on a certain piece of kit, has a particular level of reliability, and so on?
    - does it describe a system with all the required functionality, eg one that does this and that when I do this and you do that? and does it do what I expect?

How do qualification and validation relate to the tests in figure 3.1? Qualification is clearly the process of testing the System Specification against itself - arrow 4 in the figure. Validation is the process of testing the System Specification against the Requirements Expression and the user's expectations - arrow 3 in the figure.

We now take qualification and validation in turn in sections 3.3.3 and 3.3.4.

### 3.3.3    Qualifying a System Specification

In this section we identify the internal properties that we should look for in a System Specification (as opposed to the properties of what it purports to describe) and in each case look at how we can test for their presence. The section closes with a discussion of what all this tells us about the "language" in which we choose to express the System Specification.

We look at the following properties: *consistency of meaning, freedom from contradiction, unambiguity, testability, referability and feasibility.* (Not surprisingly, a number of these were relevant to the Requirements Expression too!)

*Consistency of meaning*

All words and symbols should be clearly defined (one man's jargon is another man's misunderstanding). Every word or symbol with a special or peculiar meaning in the context of the System Specification (eg of the business area concerned) should be defined in simpler terms in some way. Wherever such a defined term is used, it should be marked as such to indicate that its special meaning applies at that point.

Besides being internally consistent in its use of terms it is also important that a System Specification should be consistent with other things, in particular the Requirements Expression.

To test for consistency of meaning we can carry out the following checks:

- independent readers reviewing the System Specification can often spot inconsistent usage of terms or symbols
- comparison can be made with external glossaries (ie with other people's assumptions and frames of reference)
- concordance and cross-reference generators can provide lists of instances where terms are used; these can then be checked for consistent usage.

Whilst the clerical part of the task of checking can of course be automated, it still requires the human brain to check that the *meanings* implied in two usages of the same term are the same.

*Freedom from contradiction*

"Statements" in a System Specification can be pictorial or verbal or a mixture of the two, depending on the means of expression that we choose for the System Specification. Whatever the means, we need to be certain that the System Specification does not say one thing in one place and the opposite in another. It needs to be *internally consistent.*

There is one recurrent type of internal inconsistency that needs to be detected and avoided. This is the case where the System Specification says in one place that "X will happen in circumstances CX" and elsewhere that "Y will happen in circumstances CY". If circumstances CX and CY can overlap and actions X and Y are at odds then we have an implied contradiction.

As well as the need to remove internal contradictions, it is also important that contradictions are checked for between the System Specification and documents to which it explicitly (and implicitly) refers. The System Specification needs to be *externally consistent*. For instance, if the system being described uses data from another system then the documentation of that system should be checked to ensure that the definitions of each side of the interface match. Straightforward reading or review (qv) can be used to reveal the more obvious contradictions but for the more subtle, implied contradictions other techniques must be employed.

Contradictions can sometimes be revealed by an analysis of the state structure of the proposed system. This involves the use of Finite State Machines [Salter 1976] to model aspects of the system - the states of a process control system for instance - and then the analysis of the model to look for potential contradictions. With this technique a model (paper or computerised) is constructed that describes the system in terms of the different states that it can be in and the transitions that occur between states in response to different stimuli.

Contradictions are revealed during the construction of the model if a state (or circumstance) is found from which apparently two different state transitions can occur given the same stimulus to the system. Such a model can also be "animated" to show what the behaviour of the system would be under a certain sequence of events. This animation can reveal undesirable behaviour such as getting stuck in a particular state or circle of states. We will see later that this can be useful in detecting undesirable properties of the system implied by the definition in the System Specification.

*Unambiguity*

As with the Requirements Expression, jargon is acceptable if defined. But the danger comes when words in common usage are used in a way that has a special meaning to supplier or customer. The two sides will read the statement in two different ways and the resulting ambiguity might not be discovered until it is too late.

Testing for ambiguity can be done simply by getting the parties involved to compile a glossary of terms including especially those that sound innocent. This will throw up those terms which are given special meanings - possibly unbeknown to their users. *Data dictionaries* provide a tool-based mechanism for recording facts about systems - data dictionary products are available for most computers, from business micros through to large mainframes. They are sometimes free-standing but generally also act as front-ends to so-called *application generators*.

The System Specification should adopt and assume any "higher" glossaries that operate at, say, the user's company level and should not redefine terms locally. In particular, terms used with special meanings in the Requirements Expression should be carried over with those meanings into the System Specification. The System Specification should therefore be tested against these higher glossaries to check that there are no redefinitions, or that they are made explicit if there are any.

*Testability*

Each statement in the System Specification must be testable in the final system. This is especially important if the System Specification is part of the contractual agreement between supplier and customer. If a statement of function is untestable there will be no way for anyone to know if the suppliers have discharged their commitments.

Testing for testability is straightforward: take each statement and ask "what test would I apply to the final system in order to see whether it satisfied this statement?". Any statement for which you cannot devise an economically feasible test is an untestable statement and it must be re-expressed in a testable form or else deleted.

We can ensure testability of the System Specification right from the start simply by doing one or more of the following:

- For every "atomic" statement of function in the System Specification, an explicit test is prescribed in the System Specification itself that will be carried out on the System for Trial to check for compliance. In this case such explicit tests will of course finally be incorporated in the Acceptance Test Plan when that is written.
- For every "atomic" statement of function in the System Specification, a possible test must be outlined if not actually devised and written down. This test must be economically feasible of course. In some cases, tests might require the development of special software or hardware to check the behaviour specified in the System Specification and this will need planning and budgeting for.
- For every attribute defined in the System Specification such as the -abilities mentioned earlier, a test must be devised that will adequately check that the attribute is present in the right amount. Indeed, it is often useful to define attributes in terms of such tests.

Words such as *all, appropriate, adequate, sufficient, always, privacy, reliability, availability,* and all adverbs are often signs of an untestable statement. [Freedman 1979] gives good guidelines in this area.

*Referability*

Each "atomic" statement in the System Specification should bear some unique identifier that makes its implementation traceable throughout subsequent development and deliverables - particularly in the document describing the tests that are to form the Acceptance Test for the system.

Testing for traceability simply means ensuring by inspection that all atomic statements are clearly and uniquely labelled.

44

*Feasibility*

There is no point in specifying a system that sounds as though it will answer all of the user's prayers if it is not feasible. If you are offering to build such a system on a fixed price contract then it is positively suicidal! And if you are offering to do it on a time and materials basis then it is little better for either party.

There are a number of types of feasibility to be considered:

- Firstly and most importantly, can the system actually be built? Is it technically feasible? And is it feasible within the timescales and budgets available?
- Secondly, there is the human engineering standpoint. Will the users be able to use the proposed system? Will the system be matched to their expectations and abilities? There is no point in loading naïve users with technicalities or boring busy users with repetition in the user interface.
- Thirdly, will the system be maintainable within the maintenance timescales and budgets available?
- Fourthly, will the system be economical? Will its predicted running costs be acceptable when set against the utility value of having the system?

How do we test for these different forms of feasibility?

Technical feasibility can only be completely established by actual implementation. So, in the early days of development, checking the technical feasibility can only be done partially and to some level of confidence depending on the familiarity of the developers with the particular problem and the sort of solution that might be used. If the system involves brand new problems or still-to-be-invented solutions then an acceptable confidence level can only be achieved by a considerable amount of forward-looking design and experimentation with prototypes. Tentative checking of this sort can take the following forms:

- an outline design of the whole system is done and is itself checked for feasibility - say against similar systems successfully built in the past
- size and performance estimates are made and compared against requirements
- key algorithms are designed in detail and perhaps either implemented in a test environment or prototyped in some way.

There is clearly a danger of getting too far into the design before the System Specification is agreed since design is a costly business. The purpose of the exercise is only to ensure that there is *a* solution. This outline solution will be of use when design starts in earnest but should not unduly constrain later design work.

To test the human engineering aspects of the intended system, a frequently used technique is to produce the user interface in mock-up and have it critically reviewed by its intended users.

Ensuring the feasibility of other system attributes such as utility and maintainability requires the use of techniques such as Gilb's *Design by Objectives*. As we have seen, this involves a number of individual techniques including the decomposition of complex, unquantifiable attributes such as "maintainable" until they are expressed in terms of smaller, quantifiable attributes. The designer then identifies techniques that will ensure that they are achieved. In this way the technical feasibility of the system can be established and costs of development and maintenance checked for economic feasibility.

## 3.3.4    Validating a System Specification

We have so far tested our System Specification for certain qualities that will increase the chances that we have a "good" System Specification and that it will be a good basis for system development - the process of qualification. In this section we go on to look at how we *validate* the System Specification and to do this we take the question in two parts:

•    how do we validate the *properties* of the system that the System Specification describes?
•    how do we validate the *functions* of the system described?

The *properties* of a system are attributes such as its performance, whether it can deadlock, how quickly it responds to inputs, the amount of disc or main storage it requires to operate, and so on.

The *functions* of a system are the things that it does, generally in response to some stimulus from the outside world or some internal event. Typical functions are the display of a database record in a certain form when requested by a user, or the closing of a valve when fluid pressure drops below a certain level.

### Validating the properties of the system described

The question to be asked here is "does the System Specification describe a system with desirable properties?". We assume of course that the desirable properties are either laid down in the Requirements Expression so we can check back to that, or can be identified by users when they see them. The next question is therefore "how do we expose the properties of the system we have described?", or "how do we go about testing that the System Specification describes a system with the sort of behaviour we want?".

Firstly we need to distinguish between two sorts of properties: those that are explicitly described in the System Specification (the *explicit properties*) and those that can be deduced about the system from the description in the System Specification (the *implicit properties*). We take these separately as they need to be handled in different ways.

In the case of *explicit* properties, where for instance we have made a statement in the System Specification such as "the system must give a reply within 10 seconds", we can check whether this is what the user wants or is not. There is little more to argue about - we go to the user and the Requirements Expression and ask whether this is indeed what is required of the system.

In the case of *implicit* properties the problem is that we cannot be certain that the system we have described in words and diagrams in the System Specification will behave in the way we want. It is easy to describe a series of screen layouts on paper, how the user will get from one screen to the next, what defaults will be used and so on, but very often when such a user interface is actually developed it turns out to have quite the wrong "feel".

Similarly, we might describe a system (ie "produce a model of a system") in the System Specification and then want to test whether a system developed to satisfy that model has some desirable property or does not have some undesirable property. We want to be able to check something about the system we are specifying in terms of the model *without* having to build the system itself. For instance, the System Specification might describe a particular communication protocol to be used by the intended system - how can we be sure that the protocol will not "hang up" in certain situations or cause inappropriate actions in others?

We can check for properties *analytically* or *empirically*. Analytically we do it by deducing properties of the system from stated properties of the model using some appropriate algebra. Empirically, we do it by building a model, animating that model and checking what it does against our expectations - in some forms this is called *prototyping*.

We now look at these in turn, remembering in each case that when it comes to deciding whether a property is desirable the touchstones are the Requirements Expression and the users.

### - analytical validation

There is an increasing spread of software into areas that involve high costs in the event of failure. The cost might be in terms of human lives in the case of software controlling signalling systems or nuclear reactors. It might involve financial cost in the event of a failure in a system handling high-value transactions or a remote drilling operation. These costs have led to an increasing interest in the use of formal methods - methods with a mathematical basis - for specifying and constructing software systems. Such critical systems cannot rely on testing done in the later stages of development and formally verified specifications and designs are required to give the confidence levels required.

If a program is developed using a formal (ie mathematically based) method of specification and implementation it becomes possible to *prove* that it meets its specification. This has been done for some time now - see the work on the Gypsy system [Ambler 1977] and Euclid [Popek 1977]. But formal methods are still relatively academic, requiring mathematical expertise in their users. Commercially available courses and tools, and accessible literature are starting to become available. Nevertheless, the "industrialisation" of such methods is taking place and, despite the relatively high cost involved in training people in their use and in their actual application, they will become increasingly used in the development of critical systems particularly and perhaps of more "day-to-day" applications. Indeed a partnership of traditional testing and formal specification and development is likely to offer the confidence level required for many applications.

Formal methods operate in terms of models of the system being developed. What we can deduce or analyse about a system depends on what aspects of our intended system our model models.

Specification and design techniques such as VDM [Cohen 1986] [Jones 1980] [Jones 1986], Z [Sufrin 1985], and the Ina Jo® language [Kemmerer 1985] model the way a system operates on its data and permit mathematical proofs that a specification is (in certain senses) "correct" and that an implementation of it is also a "correct" implementation. The resulting specification includes formal expression of criteria or invariants that must be true universally or true at particular moments.

Thus, a mathematical model can be built and the required properties of the system can then be deduced as theorems. Whether or not the proven properties are "correct" - ie are those actually required by the user - is something that, as ever, only the user can decide; there is no other way of checking this.

A language such as RML (Requirements Modeling Language) [Greenspan 1984] allows the requirement and functionality of a system to be expressed formally in terms of the objects in the real world that the system is concerned with, the activities that are to take place, and assertions about the system in terms of these objects and activities.

If our model concerns state changes in the system then we will be able to deduce things about what states could be reached from other states, which states cannot be escaped from and so on. Our model might in this case be in the form of a Finite State Machine [Salter 1976].

If we are concerned about how a system specified as a number of interacting processes will behave we can use a Petri Net [Peterson 1981] [Bruno 1986] to model and analyse its dynamics. Alternatively, we might express it in terms of a formal algebra such as CSP (Cooperating Sequential Processes) [Hoare 1985] or CCS (Calculus of Communicating Systems) [Milner 1980]. In both these cases, implementation languages are available that allow a relatively direct transformation of a specification into an executable program.

If our model concerns timing relationships between the different functions of the system then we will be able to deduce things about the dynamic temporal behaviour of our system. In this case we might have produced a SPECK [Quirk 1977] [Quirk 1978] model of the system. Tools are available that allow the animation of a SPECK specification.

(® Ina Jo is a registered trademark of the System Development Corporation)

*- empirical validation*

This means building a paper or automated version of the model and "running" (animating or executing) it to see what happens.

In *prototyping*, either the entire system or some crucial part of it is constructed in a simplified form. The prototype is then run and its behaviour observed. Any undesirable behaviour or properties might be due to the simplifications made in order to be able to construct it cheaply or quickly (in which case the prototype might need to be adjusted) or might be due to an actual error in the System Specification (in which case the System Specification must of course be corrected). Prototyping is most easily done in a suitably high-level language such as APL, LISP, Prolog, me too, or with a Fourth Generation tool or language. In such languages it is possible to devise an implementation that does not require the sorts of low-level implementation decisions that have to be made when languages such as COBOL, C or Ada® are used. The me too method [Henderson 1985] allows the system specifier to create and animate a model of a proposed system in terms of the data on which it operates and the functions required on that data. See also [Henderson 1986].

In the case of a transaction processing system we might use a Fourth Generation language to build an embryonic database and to create simple versions of the screen transactions. These will allow the prospective user to use the model to check that the system's specified behaviour matches expectations and requirements, particularly in respect of properties such as usability and flexibility.

With a more formal specification of a system such as one in the form of a Finite State Machine it becomes possible to derive algorithmically a set of test cases that (in a certain sense) cover the domain of the system. Such a specification allows very strong empirical validation: we can actually exercise the model in a rigorous fashion with these test cases and decide whether the behaviour that the model exhibits is the sort of behaviour we would like to see in the real system. For instance, we can check whether any sequence of events can erroneously lead the system into a state from which it cannot escape.

The User Software Engineering methodology [Wasserman 1986] and its supporting toolset uses state machine techniques for rapid prototyping of user interfaces as part of an overall approach to the development of interactive information systems.

(® Ada is a registered trademark of the US Government (Ada Joint Program Office))

*Validating the functionality of the system described*

Having looked at the business of testing that the System Specification describes a system with the right *properties* we now consider the problem of testing that it describes a system with the right *functionality*. The test we are going to apply to the System Specification here is "does it describe a system with all and only all the required functionality?". In particular:

* is it *complete*? - does it describe all the functionality the user wants?
* is it *relevant*? - does it describe only the functionality the user wants?
* is it *correct*? - is the functionality that is described correct?

*- validating for completeness*

This means looking for holes. To do this, the user must resort to any means that could expose holes: item-by-item comparison with the Requirements Expression; discussions with people having different viewpoints of the system; reference to earlier documents relating to the system; the use of lateral thinking; and so on.

Often the methodology used in actually producing the System Specification will give help here. For instance, the CORE methodology [Mullery 1979] involves the parallel development of a description of the system from a number of different viewpoints. These are then reconciled and combined to yield a single definition of the system. Similarly, SSADM involves the parallel development of three views of a system - data flow models, "entity life history" models and entity relationship models - which are then brought together and reconciled. In the process, holes are revealed by inconsistencies between the three models.

Testing the System Specification for completeness then requires the user to pose questions about what the system would do in significant situations in their (possibly unarticulated and possibly distributed) mental model. At the same time the developer needs to identify further questions that correspond to all significant cases in the System Specification (the concrete model). The developer must then in some way - perhaps by animation - get the System Specification to answer all these questions.

If the answers generated do not correspond to the answers of the user's mental model then something is amiss. It could be the model that is at fault of course, or indeed both or neither. This needs to be decided between the user and the developer. If the System Specification is found to be wrong then it is corrected and the process continues, with earlier "tests" possibly being rerun to check that the corrections do not have unexpected side-effects.

When finally all the answers agree then we can conclude that, for the purposes of the contract at least, the System Specification is a correct description of a system that will satisfy the user's requirements as expressed in the Requirements Expression, and hence development can proceed from this agreed basis.

Problems might arise if the System Specification is expressed in some inscrutable notation. This is a problem currently being tackled by proponents of formal methods which typically involve the use of mathematical notation. To answer the questions posed by the user, the developer must interpret them in terms of the model's formalism, execute the model and then interpret the answers back into the user's frame of reference. This double translation is error-prone, involving as it does two interpretation steps. A decision therefore needs to be made as to whether the formal System Specification or the user's interpretation of it is the contractually binding form that the system must finally conform to. Ideally, given the importance of the document to the user and the utility of a formal System Specification there is much to be said for having a reader trained in the formalism on the user's team. If the nature of the application - perhaps a life-critical one - demands the use of formal methods for its correct definition then it is wrong for the final user to shirk this task simply because it is a difficult one.

Validating for completeness can of course also be helped by the qualification process described earlier. Besides giving the user and the developer the opportunity to find undesirable properties of the system being specified, empirical validation techniques offer ways of checking that all the required functionality is described in the System Specification. By showing what is described we hope to spot what is not described.

Finally, straightforward checklists can be used to good effect as reminders of the sorts of topics that should be covered in the System Specification. There are many to be found in the literature (eg [Birrell 1985]) and any organisation is advised to develop its own checklists that are peculiar to its own area of business.

### - validating for relevance

System Specifications, especially those in natural language, are prone to being clogged up with extraneous material. Authors may have good intentions and try to give background material to help the reader but the resulting collection of history, wishes for the future and justifications can only cloud the one aim of the System Specification: to express the required functionality and attributes of the system.

Whilst the System Specification is being checked for completeness, it therefore makes sense to check every statement for *relevance* as well. The testability criterion described in section 3.3.3 is a good filter for detecting irrelevant material. Of each statement in the System Specification we should ask "what test could I perform on the final system to check that this statement has been implemented?". If we cannot answer that question then it is often the case that the statement concerned is just noise! As such we might choose to leave it in the System Specification as comment (assuming it is illuminating) but we must not include it as part of the contractual content of the document.

51

*- validating for correctness*

We now have a System Specification that is consistent, unambiguous, and testable. We have covered all the aspects expected and deleted all those not expected. Is what is left *correct*? In other words, having got the bald statements right, does the System Specification *imply* anything that is not required or that is wrong? How do we go about checking this?

This is really an extension of the process of testing for completeness. Each side needs to explore the implications of the statements in the System Specification, the user using their mental model, the developer their concrete model in the System Specification.

A difficulty can arise here. To look for implications means taking combinations of statements from the System Specification and this leaves us with the traditional problem of testing something with a large number of inputs that can vary independently: "what happens if the user makes a B transaction after two A transactions?". For solutions to this problem we can look to the methods that have been devised for testing software modules, particularly those relating to "black-box" testing such as *equivalence partitioning* - see chapter 5, "The Programmer's View of Testing".

## 3.3.5   The ideal form of a System Specification

Irrespective of whether a System Specification is expressed in text, in a set of diagrams, or in a mixture of the two, we can now identify some of the desirable features of the "language" that we use for expressing it. Getting the language right is a major help in producing a testable System Specification. Experience shows that a testable System Specification is very likely to be a good System Specification on a number of other grounds. Here are some of the features that the above discussion might lead us to look for:

- *clearly identifiable keywords:* for checking the consistency of word and symbol usage and meaning; a data dictionary is a typical solution to this, or even a simple glossary
- *well-defined syntax:* for detecting ill-formed (ie potentially meaningless or ambiguous) statements
- *well-defined semantics:* for detecting (or better preventing) ambiguity and contradictions; getting everyone to understand the System Specification in the same way
- *standard formats:* wherever possible a standard form should be used for all specifications; if each specification is written in exactly the same way, with the same basic structure, checks between such documents can be more easily made and people know what to expect in a System Specification and where.

From what has been said it is clear that there are great benefits to be gained if a System Specification is expressed in a language that has some level of formality. The language can take one of three general forms, one or more of which might be used:

- *verbal* - eg English (rich but ambiguous, but see [Gowers 1986]), Structured or Tight English [Gane 1979], PSL [ISDOS 1981] and RSL [Alford 1980]
- *pictorial* - eg the data flow diagrams of Structured Analysis [Gane 1979] [Dickinson 1980], CORE diagrams, SADT™ diagrams [Ross 1977], and the state transition diagrams of Finite State Machines
- *algebraic* or *mathematical* in cases where formality is needed to help ensure correctness - eg VDM, Z, OBJ, RML, Ina Jo, CSP and CCS.

Each language allows the author to model some particular aspect(s) of a system - the data flow, the dynamic behaviour, its effect on data and so on. So the choice of language is largely determined by the type of system being specified. Indeed, it is often sensible to bring several System Specification languages to bear on different aspects of the system being modelled. The choice is also determined by the expressive power of the notation and the analytical power of the tools supporting it.

Once we are using some sort of formal language - whether it be verbal or pictorial - we have the opportunity to hold the System Specification on a computer and thereby to use computerised tools to carry out clerical checks of the sort we have described above. For instance, a System Specification in the form of text or diagrams can then be scanned by various tools that generate cross-reference tables, checklists, structure summaries, data dictionaries and so on - all things that can assist in the inspection process. REVS/RSL, PSL/PSA®, PDL/81™, MacCadd™, SPECIF, Software through Pictures™, Structured Architect™, and SA Tools are computer-based tools designed for this purpose for various methods.

(™ MacCadd is a trademark of Logica UK Limited, Software through Pictures is a trademark of Interactive Development Environments Inc., Structured Architect is a trademark of ISDOS Inc., SADT is a trademark of SofTech Inc., PDL/81 is a trademark of Caine, Farber & Gordon Inc.; ® PSL/PSA is a registered trademark of ISDOS Inc.)

## 3.4    Testing the System for Trial

### 3.4.1    Introduction

When development has finished we are left with a number of deliverables that have to be tested, and their testing intimately concerns the user of the system once more.

The main deliverable is of course the *System for Trial* and it is the testing of this object that is most important in contractual terms. This is the system that undergoes *Acceptance Testing* and results in the *Delivered System*. We will also have before us items such as user manuals and these too will need to be tested in conjunction with the System for Trial.

In section 3.1 we identified two tests of interest:

* testing that the System for Trial is a correct implementation of the System Specification
* testing that the System for Trial is correct in itself.

The process of carrying out these tests normally constitutes the *Acceptance Test*. This is the test of whether the system that has been produced matches the system agreed to with the client in the System Specification. It is a detailed set of tests that are generally described in a document known as the *Acceptance Test Plan* - see figure 2.1.

## 3.4.2   The Acceptance Test

Generally the Acceptance Test is just what is it says: if the system passes the Acceptance Test the client will accept it; if it doesn't they won't. It is not unusual for payment of some part of the contract price to be withheld until the system has passed the agreed Acceptance Test.

It is now that we realise the importance of having a System Specification that is *testable* - you will remember that this was one of the tests we applied to the System Specification itself. For now we have to write those tests. If the System Specification was well done this task will be straightforward and it will be easy for developer and user to agree what is to constitute the Acceptance Test. If it was not, this might be the time when, whilst trying to devise tests of the system, the two parties discover they have different interpretations of the System Specification. There is of course much to be said for producing the Acceptance Test Plan as soon as possible during development. Indeed, the ideal situation is for it to be produced immediately after the System Specification.

Given the System Specification how do we generate the Acceptance Test? The System Specification will in general contain three sorts of statement: statements about *functionality*, statements about *attributes*, and statements about *constraints*. These require different handling. We will first look at how they are handled in general terms and then go on to the different sorts of testing that are performed.

## 3.4.3   Testing functional statements

Well-devised functional statements will consist of *stimulus/response pairs* - statements that describe an external stimulus to be applied to the system and an observable response of the system to it. In principle, devising a test for such a statement is easy: set up a situation in which the stimulus is applied to the system under the right conditions and observe the system's response. But there are some points to note here.

Setting up the system "in the right conditions" is not always easy. (However, it must be possible or the original statement in the System Specification is untestable and hence invalid.) The situation can become difficult where the "right conditions" are the result of a period of prior running of the system. For instance, a process control system might need to display adaptive behaviour over time rather than just a response to an single event. To test this sort of behaviour will often require the use of environment simulators that can simulate *in a repeatable fashion* the environment that the system is controlling or responding to, perhaps scripted in some way.

"Observing the system's response" might also prove troublesome if that response is complex, perhaps being expressed in terms of future behaviour rather than instantaneous response, or if the system outputs large amounts of syntactically complex data. Again this might require the use of environment simulators, special recorders that can record the system's external behaviour over a period of time for subsequent analysis, and special analysis software to check the output.

Once we have sorted out these problems we can treat the derivation of Acceptance Tests for functional statements in exactly the same way as we do for the "black-box" testing of software modules - see chapter 5, "The Programmer's View of Testing".

## 3.4.4   Testing constraints

Constraints are statements such as the following which are often seen in a System Specification:

- the system must run in 1 megabyte of main storage
- the system must not use more than 20 megabytes of disc space during operation
- the system must use serial communications lines running no faster than 4800 baud
- the system must be based on the LEWSIT database management system.

Constraints are quickly dealt with in an Acceptance Test. They should simply become preconditions of the test. The environment is set up in the correct fashion or, in some cases, the system is inspected before the Acceptance Test to ensure that they are true.

## 3.4.5    Testing attributes

In this class of statements we include statements about throughput, capacity, resilience, portability, accuracy, extensibility, and so on.

We cannot test such statements unless they can be interpreted in the form of stimulus/response pairs. This might have been done at the time that the System Specification was written (the ideal situation) or it might be done now that the system exists and the statements can be interpreted in terms directly related to the actual form of the system. Quite often, an explicit test requires knowledge of implemented detail (eg of user interfaces), and this is by definition not available until we have built the system.

There is of course a potential problem of agreeing what is an adequate test of a particular performance attribute - the later this is left the more difficult it can be to agree on it!

## 3.4.6    The format of an Acceptance Test Plan

Having looked at how we decide what tests should be carried out during the Acceptance Test, we now turn to the *Acceptance Test Plan*. This is the document that will describe in detail the tests to be carried out and the results to be expected. It will generally be a detailed document formally agreed between the developer and the user.

The Acceptance Test Plan will invariably be a large document and structuring it can be a problem. Normally it will be broken down into a number of subtests and these subtests will be structured in some way. In the following table we list some of the information that we can expect to find in the Acceptance Test Plan for each subtest:

---

*Acceptance Test Plan contents for each subtest*

Subtest identification.

Cross-references back to the System Specification clauses being tested.

Personnel required and their responsibilities.

An estimated duration for the subtest (the total of all these giving a basis for estimating the time that needs to be allocated to the entire Acceptance Test).

Special hardware or software required.

Special test case generators, recording equipment or results analysers required.

Preconditions for the test (eg the successful completion of earlier subtests or the availability of test files).

The stimuli to be generated in order.
How those stimuli are to be generated.
The responses expected from the system for each of those stimuli.

The Acceptance Test Plan is often a good place to record the conduct of the Acceptance Test as agreed between the user and the supplier. The following table lists some of the issues that generally need to be covered.

*The conduct of the Acceptance Test*

What is the acceptance criterion to be applied? (eg must the system pass all the subtests or is there some level of failure that is acceptable?)
What action is to be taken if the system fails a subtest?
Is the entire Acceptance Test to be abandoned until the system is corrected or will a temporary fix be allowed so that the Test can continue?
How will such temporary fixes be reflected back into the deliverables under configuration control?
If the system has to be changed during the course of the Acceptance Test because of a failure what retesting of the system will be required after the change has been made?
What controls will there be on items that are changed as a result of the correction of failures discovered during the Acceptance Test?
Who will actually operate the system?

## 3.4.7   Testing an Acceptance Test

It is worth noting that there are a number of tests that we can apply to the Acceptance Test itself! As part of the process of agreeing it, it should be checked for completeness and feasibility. Completeness can be checked by referring back to the System Specification and ensuring that all statements have been thoroughly tested. A feasible Acceptance Test is one that is practicable in technical terms, in terms of the cost to carry it out and in terms of the resources required.

In some cases we have seen that special software, hardware, or other equipment might be necessary to support the Acceptance Testing. This must be planned and budgetted for and scheduled so that it is ready well before the Acceptance

Test itself - in fact it is very likely to be required during the Integration Testing and System Testing described in chapter 4.

# Chapter 4 - The Designer's View of Testing

## 4.1   The system design process

The System Design phase of the development life-cycle is the transition between the System Specification and Module Design and Implementation activities. We define the system design process as follows:

*System design* is the process of defining the division of a system into subsystems and components, or directly into components. The external function and interface of each component and subsystem are specified, and an explanation is given as to how the components are combined into subsystems and thence into the system to provide an implementation of the System Specification.

The main functions of a system designer are therefore:

1    to decide upon the individual parts of the system, perhaps logical groupings of operations or functional groupings as determined from examination of the System Specification
2    to identify and specify system- or subsystem-wide data entities
3    to document the chosen partition of the system and explain the rationale for the split and the way in which the assembled parts will function to provide a complete implementation
4    to provide documentation for each component so that it can be implemented
5    to specify the hardware and implementation language to be used and justify the choice (unless it is constrained by the Requirements Expression or System Specification).

There are a variety of methods that assist the designer in stages 1 and 2, such as JSD [Jackson 1983], SSADM, and Object Oriented Design [Booch 1986].

Stage 3 should follow on almost mechanically from the previous two stages. (If it doesn't then there may well be a better, more "intuitive" way to split the system.)

Stage 4 is achieved by describing precisely the external specification of each component, the global data objects acted upon (either read or written to) and a precise definition of the overall function of the component. Algorithmic details must be "mind-sized" and specified in a language with well-defined semantics. Formal methods are beginning to be employed at this stage, having the benefit of producing unambiguous specifications of the components.

Stage 5 has two parts:

- Determining the hardware requirements imposed by the System Specification, ie compatibility considerations, expansion capability, performance requirements, data storage requirements, failure rate constraints etc.
- Investigating the specifications of available hardware to produce a short-list of satisfactory systems. The final choice is then made by determining the "most suitable" system: this may entail benchmarking, financial considerations, performance guarantees from the hardware supplier, availability, maintenance costs, development tool availability etc.

It is well known that the System Design phase is crucial to the success or failure of a project. A poor choice of system partition, hardware, or development language can lead to disasters: once one is committed to an architecture that proves unsuitable it is very expensive to rectify it.

Figure 4.1 shows the fragment of our life-cycle model that relates to the Designer's View. We can see that the system design process takes as its input the System Specification and produces a design for a system in terms of specifications of software components or modules. The latter constitute what we call here the *System Design Specification*. Once these components have been produced and individually tested (as described in chapter 5) they re-enter the sphere of concern of the designer. They must now be integrated and tested to form the complete system in a state ready for transfer to Acceptance Testing as the *System for Trial*. This is the deliverable of this part of the life-cycle.

Testing from the designer's viewpoint therefore has the following components:

- testing that the System Design Specification describes a system that will correctly implement the System Specification (arrow 1)
- testing that the System Design Specification is correct in itself (arrow 2)
- testing that the software components correctly integrate and implement the System Design Specification (arrows 3 and 4).

In section 4.2 we look at the first two of these components which relate to testing the design. In section 4.3 and 4.4 we look at the third component, dividing it into *integration testing* and *system testing* respectively.

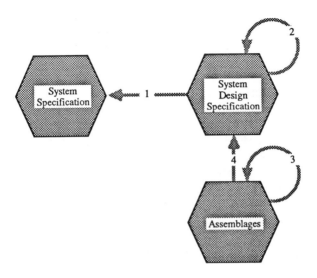

Figure 4.1 - The designer's view of the life-cycle

## 4.2 Testing the design

### 4.2.1 What to test for in a system design

The System Design Specification must be tested to ensure that it is:

- *complete*: it must address all of the identified system functions in the System Specification, ie each statement in the System Specification must be traceable to those parts of the System Design Specification that prescribe its implementation; there must be no missing details such as partial or non-existent references and no places where decisions have not been fully explained or have been left to be decided; ideally there should be strong cross-referencing between the System Design Specification and the System Specification to ensure completeness.
- *consistent*: there must not be any conflicting usage of either internally or externally specified operations on data items; timing constraints, if present, should be non-contradictory; again, to help consistency, each statement in the System Design Specification should be traceable back to the associated System Specification statements(s) which it implements.
- *testable*: it must be possible to devise pass/fail test cases for each System Design Specification statement, ie it must be possible to determine whether an implementation does indeed satisfy the System Design Specification.

- *feasible*: it must specify a system that can be produced within economically justifiable costs, ie the benefit to be accrued outweighs the development costs; there must be little or no risk that the development will not be completed within the planned costs.

These four desirable properties of a System Design Specification have been established for some time and modern design techniques offer techniques for producing designs with these qualities and for checking for them during the production process.

The completeness and consistency properties are obviously essential for a successful implementation. The check for testability ensures that the System Design Specification contains sufficient design detail for each module to constrain the developers to a single, unambiguous interpretation of the designer's intent. The risk assessment in the feasibility test exercise must not be overlooked! Experience has shown that projects which do not identify and resolve risks at design time can fail and fail badly.

The following table summarises the areas of the System Design Specification that are to be tested. Subsequent sections deal with test methods that can be applied to these areas.

---

*Desirable design properties*

*Completeness*
- it addresses all items in the System Specification
- there are no references to non-existent or incomplete documents
- there are no decisions left unmade

*Consistency*
- there is no conflicting usage of internal, external or operational items
- there are no contradictory response times
- each design decision is traceable back to System Design Specification statements

*Feasibility*
- the design is technically possible
- it makes realistic demands on human support
- required hardware performance and capacity are not close to specification limits
- there is sufficient leeway or mechanisms for foreseeable growth

- the design has maintenance in mind
- there are no major risk issues

*Testability*
- it is possible to devise pass/fail tests for all design statements

---

## 4.2.2 Test methods for a system design

The main, and in practice, often the only test method is manual inspection. This may take the form of informal reviews by various concerned individuals or, more effectively, organised reviews along the lines of the Fagan or Parnas methods - see for instance [Fagan 1976] [IBM/1]. The method described in [Parnas 1985] offers a benefit over the Fagan method by forcing reviewers to adopt a viewpoint and to study the design in some detail. Yourdon's structured walkthroughs [Yourdon 1979] present a similar role-based approach (see section 3.2.3 above). Freedman and Weinberg offer substantial checklists in their *Review Handbook* [Freedman 1979]. Each organisation should adopt one of these methods or some combination of them.

Such reviews, supplemented by modelling or prototyping to prove feasibility, can be very effective in error detection. These reviews are most effective if the proper focus is applied and the following discussions about System Design Specification properties and applicable test methods should guide you.

Increasingly, formal methods are providing ways of testing design. Both VDM and Z offer techniques for developing a design and an implementation that are correct inasmuch as they can be proved mathematically to implement a formally described specification. See the literature referred to in chapter 3.

*Testing for completeness*

A manual inspection should be made to ensure that each lowest level System Specification statement is dealt with in the System Design Specification - in other words that the System Design Specification is *externally complete*. To help in this check it is desirable that these System Design Specification statements are labelled - once again the notion of "referability".

All decisions must have been made and there should be no loose ends that might lead to misinterpretation or holes in the implementation. For example statements such as *the database interface function DBI_F will set an error flag indicating the sort of error found*, and *the module PROCESS_TOOL_RESPONSE will parse data from the machine tool* are symptoms of an incomplete design. In the first case we need to answer the questions: "where is the error flag?", "what are the possible sorts of error which can be encountered?" and "why is there to be an error flag anyway?". In the second case we need to know the form of the incoming data, the frequency and volume of such data and what needs to be done to the data.

The reviewers must also ensure that references either within the System Design Specification or to external documents do actually exist and that they supply the necessary detail of information. External references must be approved and controlled documents that reflect the true state of the external items to be used. Otherwise we have a "risk".

### Testing for consistency

We need to check that there are no conflicts in data usage, incorrect calls upon existing operations or performance or timing incompatibilities. We take these in turn.

Considering firstly the data usage tests, modules will ideally share only a minimal amount of data - in other words they will be *loosely coupled*. We must therefore ensure that any shared data really ought to be shared. For situations where data must be shared it should be clearly specified as *global* or *shared* together with the list of modules that read, set, or read and set the data item.

The sorts of inconsistencies that can arise are:

- the use of uninitialised data items
- an intervening, unexpected change of value by a second process prior to the use of the data item by the first process
- deadly embrace situations where several processes are waiting for a data item to attain a certain value (these processes being the sole ones which access the particular data item)
- the attempted access of de-allocated dynamic data items
- lost updates where two processes both change an item believing they are the only one doing it.

Automated mechanisms that can perform such checks on a design generally rely on the designer first building a *model* of their design and then carrying out analyses on the model. The tool support identified in chapter 3 for the analytical testing of System Specifications is frequently applicable to designs, especially high-level designs. Diagramming tools, data dictionary tools, finite state modelling tools etc often allow the designer to make the sorts of consistency checks listed above.

At the more detailed level of design procedure, subroutine or function calls must correspond to their specification. This check can be automated, and indeed certain more modern languages such as Ada have been designed to force a split between an operation's *signature* or specification and its implementation. If the implementation is to use such a language then it is desirable to specify the actual signatures in the design, so that the compiler can be used as a design validation aid. If used to capture design, strongly typed languages are useful in that compilers for them can check for type inconsistencies that, even in less strongly typed languages, would slip through and need to be found by dynamic testing.

A simple check that can sometimes reveal the presence of inconsistencies is to compare the name of a unit of software with its actual function. During design, names will tend to remain the same whilst changes in functionality frequently occur. As the two diverge so might the actual function of a software unit and the function expected of it by another unit.

Some designs, for real-time applications for instance, must define the requisite response constraints for each module. In such cases we must ensure that the response time for a calling module is greater than the cumulative response times for the modules called (assuming we are using standard sequential hardware). The testing of parallel processing designs for timing consistency requires mathematical models - traditional modelling methods can be applied and tool support is often available for them. Advice on such design testing is beyond the scope of this book except to say that such testing must be performed before large sums of money are committed to implementation.

The System Design Specification must not contain any embellishments or unnecessary detail. The cross-reference of System Design Specification statements back to their antecedents in the System Specification serves to ensure that this is so. (If it is thought that there should be some additional function in the System Specification then the System Specification itself should be questioned and, if necessary, amended under version control.)

### Testing for feasibility

A design is feasible if the life-cycle benefit of the system exceeds the life-cycle costs. In other words, not only does the system have to be technically possible it must also be financially viable.

The life-cycle costs can be estimated by using historical data on similar developments or by some form of life-cycle model. See for instance [Putnam 1978] and [IBM/2].

Life-cycle benefits can be assessed by calculating the savings to be achieved, or the likely increase in turnover, from the availability of such a system. It follows that any development risk areas must be identified and resolved at this juncture. Risks occur in the following forms:

- *technical*: is the development of such systems well understood? The production of the first FORTRAN compiler was considered by some to be almost impossible whilst nowadays such a development would not present any major difficulties. Technical complexity in a design might be a symptom of the fact that the design is poorly understood or lacking conceptual clarity.

- *hardware*: will the specified hardware provide the data storage and performance anticipated? Is the hardware available? If it is under development what risk is there that it will not fulfil its specification or perform to its maximal capacity?

- *human factors*: will the system prove satisfactory to its users? Is the human computer interface (HCI) suitable for the intended user community? Is the predicted response time acceptable? Are the tasks and skills expected from operators and users realistic?

- *performance*: are there any areas where the anticipated performance will be near to the limit allowed in the System Specification? If so, slight variance here may cause a failure.

- *reliability*: will the system have the prescribed reliability, eg tolerance to component failure?

- *scale complexity*: the degree of difficulty for developments increases exponentially with the project size - see Brooks's "The Mythical Man-Month" [Brooks 1975]. Estimates should take this factor into account. There are some automated and manual support aids, which, in the absence of detailed statistics of similar developments, should be used to produce "best possible" time and cost estimates - see in particular Boehm's COCOMO cost estimating model [Boehm 1981].

- *future expectations*: any useful system is expanded to cater for additional needs after some time in service. It is wise to provide enough spare capacity and generalisation to accommodate perceived future requirements. In other words, we have a risk if the system cannot be realistically or easily expanded.

We try to detect such areas of risk initially by manual examination of the design. It may prove sensible to "model" the system in some fashion to actually determine whether a risk does exist. For instance, HCI uncertainties can be resolved by simulating the interface and allowing users to perform an evaluation. Technical risk can be resolved by actually prototyping the areas of technical difficulty in advance of any large scale development. Hardware risks can be reduced by benchmarking existing systems. If the hardware to be used is not yet fully developed then some security can be had by seeking guarantees of performance, data storage, address space etc.

*Testing for testability*

Each atomic System Design Specification statement is considered in turn and tests are devised that, for a realistic cost, would show up an erroneous implementation that does not fulfil the design. If it proves difficult to devise such tests then more precise detail is required as to what is intended.

66

For example, in both of the following cases we would need to be mind-readers to understand the designer's intent:

- "The procedure XYZ will provide a result within an acceptable time period"
- "The user interface function GETIO will support several simultaneous interactive users".

When designs are compared, it is usually clear that some are inherently more testable than others. Below we give some lists of the factors that lead to high or low testability. Moreover, the testability of a design changes over time with the addition or amendment of requirements and conditions, so we also look briefly at this capacity for degeneration.

Firstly, what things happen during design that can increase testability? In the following table we identify some of these.

---

*Design factors leading to high testability*

Retention of initial and intermediate factors in calculations.
Provision of alternative routines for high-risk factors.
Provision for traceability, restart, progress recording and reporting.
Simplicity of design leading to minimum activity strings for the performance of functions.
Simplicity of design documentation leading to ease of access to and understanding of the documentation.
Visibility of actions at interfaces.
Early consideration during the design process of error containment, recovery and reporting.
Single-purpose use of common routines and storage areas.
Highly separated concerns where activities operate independently.

---

Next, what sorts of bad practices cause us to produce designs of low testability?

---

*Design factors leading to low testability*

High priority requirements for compactness, efficiency and speed.
Multi-purpose usage of common routines and storage areas.

---

Highly "integrated" activities in which each action depends on the outcomes of previous activities.

Complex designs and long activity strings.

"Clever" designs.

Low priority put on timely and effective documentation.

Concentration at early stages on the "normal case", with the handling of errors and unusual situations added on to the design.

Lack of sufficient data or design studies on the quality, quantity and interactions to be expected in "real" use.

An initially acceptable level of testability can degenerate during the development of a design. Some of the causes are given in the table below.

*Causes of the degeneration of a design*

Unbalancing of the design due to random additions and alterations.

Reluctance to consider redefinition of the problem, and redesign, after a certain amount of work has gone into the first attempt.

Failure to assign the correct priorities to new requirements ("newest" is not necessarily "most important").

Failure to distinguish between what is vital (for example, maintaining a clean, testable and clearly documented design) from what is currently interesting (possibly contriving to squeeze more functionality or performance out of the design than it can comfortably provide).

The design is the pivot of the development of a system. It marks the transition from theory to tangible outcome. Controlling its testability is essential for an acceptable result, and the means available are reviews, simulations, the application of metrics, and pilot implementations and trials of sections of the design. It is recommended that all four are used in every case. How is each related to testability?

- *Reviews.* Demonstration and investigation tests should be developed in parallel with the functional design, and used with relevant scenarios in reviewing whether testing can be undertaken satisfactorily. Estimates of the efficiency and resource costs, as well as requirements for special testing support tools, can be identified with reasonable accuracy at early stages of design and used with the other elements of the review to assess viability and guide system development strategies.

- *Simulations* (whether paper-, person- or machine-based) are a powerful tool for investigating testability because they focus attention on the interfaces between design elements and thus on the data and commands that will cross them and that must be tested. Interface investigations also direct our attention to demonstrations of performance, and to considerations of the diagnostic facilities that will be needed both for testing and for in-service support.

- *Application of metrics.* The particular metrics used, and whether they are extracted mechanically or manually, will depend on the design methods and documentation methods being used. However, although it is not yet possible to prescribe the best metric for every situation, it is clear that there are simple measures related to complexity, coupling and cohesion which can be used to guide the decision to accept or reject a design on the grounds of its difficulty to test, to modify and to understand. A description of these can be found in chapter 5.

- *Pilot implementations and trials.* Depending on the system and the way in which it is being designed, it may either be possible to implement one or more whole functions, or be necessary to create a cut-down version of the entire product. In either case, much useful information on the nature and performance of the design can be obtained, as well as an assessment of its testability in general. The testability should be approached by following normal development standards, creating tests in parallel with the system and applying them as soon as the appropriate object exists. Pilots and trials should give an accurate answer as to the availability and adequacy of the system's and project's test support requirements.

## 4.3    Integration testing

### 4.3.1    Introduction

During the design stage of the software life-cycle, high-level software structures and data structures are specified. Typical software structures are processes (schedulable items), object libraries, macro libraries, and command files. The purpose of integration testing is to prove that the implementation of those high-level structures provides the functionality, performance and reliability required of them (individually and collectively) in the System Design Specification.

In summary, integration testing takes as its input modules that have been checked out by module testing, groups them in larger and larger aggregates, applies the tests defined in an Integration Test Plan to those aggregates, and delivers as its end product an integrated system ready for trial - see figure 4.1.

69

We first do some scene setting for integration testing by recapping on activities during preceding life-cycle stages and by defining some terms.

The high-level software structures specified during the design stage were decomposed into specifications of lower-level software structures. The lower-level specifications then became the specifications for the module design stage of the life-cycle. We call the high-level software structures *assemblages* and the low-level structures *components*. A component will yield one or more software *modules*.

Clearly there is an interface between module testing and integration testing. The unit of transfer across that interface may consist of either a tested module, a tested component or a tested assemblage depending on the module testing philosophy employed, namely with modules being tested in isolation or incrementally to component or assemblage level.

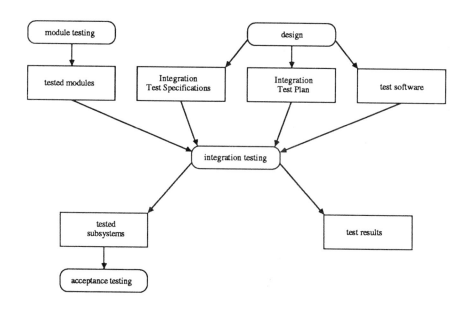

Figure 4.2 - Integration testing

Integration testing is performed in accordance with an *Integration Test Plan*. The Integration Test Plan is produced during the design stage of the life-cycle and defines the strategy of the integration testing activity. An *Integration Test Specification* is produced for each integration test. This defines in detail how software structures are to be combined for testing, the prerequisites of the test, the step by step operation of the test, and the expected results as defined in the design specification of the software under test. The execution of a test will produce a set of actual results. By comparing the actual and expected results we can verify whether the software under test performs according to its design specification.

There is also an interface between integration testing and system testing. The major output of integration is a tested system or, in some cases, a set of tested subsystems, eg a subsystem for the main processor and a subsystem for each peripheral processor.

A pictorial view of integration testing is given in figure 4.2. Note that all interfaces with integration testing are channelled through files under Configuration Management control.

## 4.3.2   The scope of integration

As we can see from the above introduction, the scope of integration testing is dependent on several factors:

- the size and complexity of the software
- the hardware configuration on which the software is to run
- the philosophy of module testing
- the availability of tools on host and target machines.

The scope should be tied down in the Integration Test Plan. This is produced towards the end of the design stage. At that time the factors listed above should have been defined and will therefore be available for use in the planning of integration testing.

## 4.3.3   The objectives of integration

The objective of integration testing is to verify the functional, performance and reliability requirements placed on major design items, ie assemblages. The assemblages are exercised through their interfaces using black-box testing (qv), with success and error cases being simulated through appropriate parameter and data inputs. Simulated operational usage of shared data areas and inter-process communication or synchronisation is tested. Individual subsystems are exercised through their input interfaces. Test cases are constructed to test that components within an assemblage interact correctly, for instance across procedure calls or process activations.

71

The overall approach is the "building block" approach in which verified assemblages are added to a verified base which is then used to support the integration testing of further assemblages.

### 4.3.4    The organisation of integration

Ideally integration testing is carried out by a team that is independent of the programming team. The relationship between the integration team and the programming team should be one of customer and supplier. The interface between them should be formal, ie controlled by formal Configuration Management procedures. Units of tested software are only accepted by the integration team from Configuration Management on controlled media. The programming team are only allowed to register software with Configuration Management if it has achieved the level of quality required by the project standards (typically the module meets its specification). Thus the integration team can have a reasonable level of confidence in the software they have to handle.

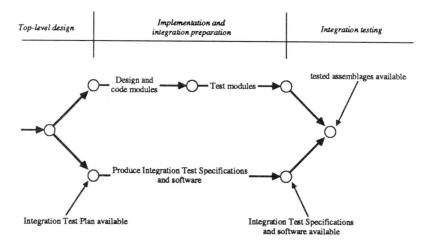

Figure 4.3  -  An overview of integration testing

Part of the documentation produced during the design stage will cover the approach to integration testing, and consists of:

- the Integration Test Plan, which defines the method and order of integration testing
- the assemblage specifications and interface specifications, which define functional, performance and reliability requirements on the design.

The Integration Test Plan should be a joint venture between the design team and the integration team. The document is tested by review (see section 4.3.5 below). In parallel with the module design and test stages the integration team produces the Integration Test Specifications and the test software for each test identified in the Integration Test Plan. These documents are also reviewed (see section 4.3.6 below). The integration tests are then executed as the assemblages are released by the module testers.

Obviously, there must be planning co-ordination between the assemblage production and integration testing activities. Figure 4.3 shows the typical planning model for integration test preparation and execution.

## 4.3.5    The Integration Test Plan

*Drawing up the Integration Test Plan*

The purpose of the Integration Test Plan is to define the strategy of the integration testing activity in terms of the order of integration, the tests to be performed, the hardware on which the tests are to be run and the tools and procedures to be employed.

We recommend the following contents list for an Integration Test Plan, although your own might not necessarily be in the same format. For a system consisting of several subsystems, a separate section 3 (or equivalent) is suggested for each subsystem.

---

*The contents of an Integration Test Plan*

1        *Introduction and Organisation*
- introduces the document
- describes the organisation in terms of the procedures to be followed and the tools and hardware available to the integration team

2  *Strategy*

    &deg; identifies the end product(s) of integration testing, eg the tested system or tested subsystems

    &bull; identifies the Integration Test Specifications to be produced

    &deg; outlines the purpose of each integration test

    &deg; defines the order in which the integration tests are to be performed

3  *Integration Test Specification Contents*

    &deg; for each Integration Test Specification mentioned in the Strategy, defines the assemblage(s) under test and the design requirements which are to be verified

    &bull; identifies the hardware configuration required for the test

    &bull; lists the tools and test software

    &bull; identifies previously tested assemblages necessary for the test

---

*Testing the Integration Test Plan*

The Integration Test Plan should be formally reviewed by the following parties:

- *management*: what should be the schedule for testing? what activities need to be planned for the development of special software and hardware?
- *design team*: will the Integration Test Plan provide a good strategy for verifying the implementation of design requirements?
- *programming team*: is the order of testing assemblages required by the Integration Test Plan feasible in the timescales given the skills and resources available?
- *integration team*: is the testing schedule feasible considering the availability of skills, tools and hardware?
- *acceptance team*: is the Integration Test Plan capable of producing an acceptable product for the team to receive?
- *Quality Assurance*: does the plan meet the quality requirements of the project?

The criteria used to assess the Integration Test Plan during the review are:

- *completeness*
    - are all design requirements included?
    - are all assemblages and interfaces tested?
- *feasibility*
    - will resources be available when required?
    - will the stated resources be adequate?
    - can the programming team support the required order and timescales of assemblage production?
    - where parallelism is built into the plan can the integration team support it and are there sufficient hardware and software resources to support it?
- *consistency*
    - is the order of testing consistent in that a base of integrated and tested assemblages is always used to support the software under test?

When the Integration Test Plan has passed its review, it is placed under Configuration Management control. It then becomes the driving document for the next phase of the preparation for integration testing, ie the production of the Integration Test Specifications.

## 4.3.6   Integration Test Specifications

*Drawing up an Integration Test Specification*

An Integration Test Specification expands the summary included in section 3 of the Integration Test Plan and provides the precise conditions, operations and procedures that will verify the assemblages against referenced design requirements in a repeatable and consistent manner.

The following contents list is a suggested format. The contents themselves should be included in any Integration Test Specification.

---

*The contents of an Integration Test Specification*

*Introduction*
- introduces the document
- identifies the assemblages to be tested
- outlines the parts of the System Design Specification to

be verified

*Requirements*
* identifies all design requirements to be verified

*Test Software Specifications*
o gives detailed specifications from which test software (drivers, tracers, data reducers, results analysers etc) can be implemented (note that specification, design and coding standards for the product software can apply here)
* explains interactions with existing tools
o specifies software for the Set Up, Test Execution and Close Down Procedures

*Configuration*
* identifies the hardware and software configuration on which the software under test and the test software will be loaded
* defines and justifies values for any user-definable parameters of the configuration
* identifies restrictions on the use of the configuration during the test, eg the tester must be the sole user, no other users to access line printer 2, etc
* defines the numbers and types of operators, supervisors and observers and allocates their roles

*Set Up Procedure*
* describes the procedure for bringing the configuration (hardware, software and personnel) into a state of readiness in which the execution of the test can begin
o consists of a step-by-step list of observable operations with a results/comment column for observations to be recorded

*Test Execution Procedure*
* defines the step-by-step execution of the test
* typically consists of a table containing the following columns:
  a an identifier of the step
  b the operations to be performed, either by a person or a piece of test software
  c the expected results of the operation
  d design requirement identification(s) if the step

76

                        does in fact test a particular requirement(s)

   e        an observations column in which the appearance or non-appearance of the expected results can be recorded (note that some results can only be observed during post test analysis - this should be indicated in column (c); this is primarily intended for the use of Quality Assurance observers during formal test runs

*Close Down Procedure*
- defines the step-by-step procedure for closing down the test configuration and for the storage and retrieval of results
- includes steps to:
    - stop the test run
    - close any results files still open
    - organise hard copies of results
    - return the configuration to the state in force before the Set Up Procedure

*Results Checking*
- describes how the results are to be checked (simply observable results are covered in the Test Execution Procedure section above)
- provides operating instructions for automated data reduction and results analysis programs
- where results are a function of unpredictable variables (eg time), provides the algorithms necessary to check the results

---

*Testing an Integration Test Specification*

An Integration Test Specification should be formally reviewed by the following parties:

- *design team*: does the Integration Test Specification provide the capability of verifying the satisfaction of the design requirements?
- *integration team:* are the tests feasible?
- *Quality Assurance:* does the Integration Test Specification comply with project standards?

The major review criteria are:

- *completeness*
    - are all appropriate design requirements included?
    - are the test cases sufficient to verify the design requirements of the System Design Specification (see section 4.3.7)?
    - are all interfaces of the software under test exercised?
- *consistency*
    - are more resources required than planned for in the Integration Test Plan?

When the Integration Test Specification has been successfully reviewed, it can be placed under Configuration Management control. Any necessary test software or hardware can then be developed.


### The conduct of an Integration Test

During the development of an integration test, the procedural sections of the Integration Test Specification (Set Up, Test Execution, Close Down and Results Checking) should be followed faithfully whenever possible. This will ensure that any inter-step dependencies are preserved. A full scale rehearsal of the complete test execution should be undertaken at the end of the test development. The two measures above should ensure that the formal test run will not produce any unfortunate surprises. Test software should be placed under Configuration Management control after a successful rehearsal so that a controlled build can be made for the formal run.

A test manager should be appointed for the formal run. This person has the following responsibilities:

- the provision of configuration details for the Integration Team and Quality Assurance records
- the step-by-step control of the procedural sections of the Integration Test Specification, allowing sufficient time for observations to be noted, steps to be synchronised and ensuring that deviations from the procedural section do not occur
- the provision of copies of actual and expected results to the Integration Team and Quality Assurance
- the production of a test report that:
    - names the personnel involved
    - gives the success status of the test
    - provides a statement agreed with the Design and Integration Teams and QA concerning any deviations from expected results supported by Software Problem Reports.

At the end of a formal run the actual results should be retained under Configuration Management control.

## 4.3.7   Test software

Special test software may be required to support some of the integration tests. The specification of any such software should appear in an Integration Test Specification. All test software should be produced using the same standards as those used in the production of the actual system as it too will be used and changed during the maintenance of the system.

Of major concern to the integration team is the software that applies test cases during the Test Execution Procedure. It is on the test cases that the design verification will depend. The test cases must be chosen methodically so that they do not proliferate to an unmanageable volume whilst at the same time achieving adequate test coverage. The criterion of testing of all paths and all conditions (see *coverage criteria*) can lead to an astronomical number of test cases for module testing, and so it is clearly impractical for integration testing where the number of paths and conditions can be orders of magnitude greater.

Integration testing is concerned with the verification of the specification of design items. It involves verifying that independently implemented units work together in the way intended by the System Design Specification. This generally restricts integration testing to *black-box* testing inasmuch as the construction of test cases for assemblages does not involve looking inside the units forming the assemblage. This will have been done when those units were tested at Unit Testing time (see chapter 5). As such, the techniques used for black-box test case derivation in module testing are equally applicable. These are described in [Myers 1979] and [Beizer 1983] and are summarised below. However, there is an important sense in which *white-box* testing is applicable to integration and we will start with this.

### *White-box testing of assemblages*

In an assemblage of components there will be some form of control structure operating between them: this might take the form of a module calling hierarchy (as would result from the use of Structured Design methods), an object message-passing network (as would result from the use of object-oriented design), a process or task network (as would result from a multi-process design reached using, say, the MASCOT design method), or indeed a combination of several of these. The aim of white-box testing in these situations is to exercise a "representative" set of control paths through these networks and hierarchies and this will involve examination of the conditions needed to cause them to occur. See section 5.3.4 for an outline of white-box testing techniques.

*Equivalence partitioning*

Equivalence partitioning is a black-box testing technique concerned with identifying classes of inputs over which the behaviour of the software is "similar". For example, suppose a software item is specified to behave in one way if an input item takes the integer values 1 through to 10 inclusive and another way for values outside that range. Then, for that item, there are three input equivalence classes: 1 through 10, all integers less than 1 and all integers greater than 10. The hypothesis of equivalence partitioning is that if we select a representative value of the first class of inputs (eg 5) and if the software under test reacts according to its specification for 5, then it will do so for all values in that class. A similar argument applies to representative values of the other two classes (eg 0 and 22). Test cases can then be derived using 5, 0, and 22 as being representative of the three classes.

*Boundary-value analysis*

Boundary-value analysis is a technique closely related to equivalence partitioning. It concentrates on those values within equivalence classes that normally attract a large number of errors. These are the boundaries of the equivalence classes. Applying boundary-value analysis to the example above would result in test cases for values 0, 1, 10, and 11 of the input item. Although this results in an increase in the number of test cases, the most error-prone values are exercised and hence the efficiency of the testing can be increased.

Boundary-value analysis can also be applied to output values. Test cases can be devised which generate output values at the boundaries of valid equivalence classes. It may well be productive to attempt to generate output values in the invalid equivalence classes.

*Cause-effect graphing*

Equivalence partitioning and boundary-value analysis do not support the design of test cases that investigate the operation of the software when combinations of input conditions are applied. Cause-effect graphing is a method of designing a relatively small number of test cases to test combinations of input conditions, where a *cause* is an input condition and an *effect* is an output condition. A graph is drawn which shows the transformations necessary to achieve the effects from the causes according to the functionality expressed in the design specification.

Even though cause-effect graphing is an efficient way of deriving representative test cases from a potentially huge set of combinations, it does become unwieldy very quickly unless large specifications can be subdivided.

*Error guessing*

Based on experience and/or intuition, the test case designer identifies the most likely sources of error, eg contention for resources, resources empty or full, and non-initialised items.

*Testing performance and reliability requirements*

A part of the specification of the test software is the definition of test cases. The adequacy of the test cases will be a major topic of the review done on the Integration Test Specification. It is therefore advisable to adopt a methodical approach to test case design. The recommended approach is to use the techniques described above, in the order in which they are described, to achieve a comprehensive set of test cases.

It is all too easy to concentrate on functional requirements when designing test cases, but integration testing is also concerned with the verification of performance and reliability requirements. The test case design techniques are equally applicable to performance requirements. Test cases can be derived which test up to and including performance limits. Others can be derived which exceed the performance limits to find the point at which the system collapses; in this way we can determine how close the reliability of the system is to its required performance.

For example, suppose an operating system design has a performance requirement that it must allow up to $n$ concurrently executing processes. This requirement may be implemented in the design of more than one assemblage - the global data area must be large enough to hold the housekeeping data for $n$ processes and the "create process" system service must not allow an $n+1$th process to be created. Test cases to create $n$ processes and $n+1$ processes will verify that the performance requirement has been met and prove that the software reacts in the required manner to an attempt to overload the global data area (eg an error report is returned to the user and their request for some system service is denied).

Performance requirements can also relate to required rates of work. For example, the software assemblages supporting the human computer interface might have to be able to provide a response time of half a second while serving ten operators, each entering strings of characters at a rate of four characters per second. A test case to reflect these stated conditions would verify the performance requirement. By adding an extra operator, or by increasing the typing rate of one or more of the existing operators, a state of service maintained at a lower performance can be demonstrated - a typical performance/reliability requirement which demands graceful degradation rather than complete loss of service.

Reliability requirements are varied in flavour. They cover required reaction to stress conditions, failure recovery and continuous operation. One of the examples above demonstrates an important aspect of reliability in that service is maintained albeit at a lower level of performance. Reliability can be summarised as maintaining a service under adverse conditions and maintaining a normal service under normal continuous operational conditions. Test cases to prove the reliability requirements of software must generate these conditions. For example:

- taking down a processing node to demonstrate the introduction of a warm standby and the re-establishment of normal service with no loss of data
- demonstration of the software to handle power fail recovery by switching off the machine
- the soak testing of software under normal operational conditions to search for errors that either require time to appear (such as the slow but continual depletion of disc space because of a faulty de-allocation mechanism) or only happen under rare circumstances.

## 4.4    System testing

Once all of the software assemblages have been integrated and the integrated software system itself integrated with any hardware subsystems, the time has come to carry out *system testing*. Integration testing sought to detect inconsistencies between the software assemblages, or between software assemblages and hardware. System testing is the limiting case and seeks to detect both types of inter-assemblage inconsistency by exercising the complete system.

System testing is the first time at which the entire system can be tested against the System Specification - the document that says what it should do. As such, system testing is a form of *black-box testing*. Acceptance Testing is a form of *demonstrative testing* where we aim to demonstrate that the system behaves correctly. In contrast, we can expect system testing to be more *investigatory*, where we aim to be more destructive in our attitude to test case design and we explore the behaviour of the system up to and beyond the bounds defined in the System Specification.

So we can view system testing as the final destructive phase of integration testing and a preamble to the demonstrative Acceptance Testing. We have seen how Acceptance Testing involves not just the software and hardware forming the System for Trial but also all of the user documentation that will accompany it - the User Guide, Reference Manuals and so on.

In the following sections we identify a variety of different sorts of testing that should be considered for the system. They are designed to exercise the system as thoroughly as possible both inside its design envelope and also outside. Clearly, if it does not work outside its design envelope this might not be considered a "failure" of the system but it might well point to a weakness in it or to some aspect that is running perilously close to a required value.

*Functional testing*

This is of course the bulk of System and Acceptance Testing and it involves the derivation of black-box tests on the system from the System Specification. Many of the techniques that are used for deriving tests of software modules can be used here - equivalence partitioning, boundary-value analysis, cause-effect graphing and so on (see section 4.3.7 above and chapter 5). For a system specified and designed using Structured Analysis, [McCabe 1985] describes a technique for deriving system test cases from the data flow diagrams used in the original system analysis.

*User interface testing*

Firstly the User Guide must be checked against the System Specification and perhaps against the Requirements Expression. The user interfaces are then tested using the User Guide and System Specification together to find areas where they do not comply with stated functionality or where the User Guide does not describe the interface correctly or in sufficient detail.

Tests of invalid input and flagrant attempts to break the system must be created. The experience of the tester comes to the fore here. Tests must also be devised to probe for conformance with agreed standards. The interface must be evaluated for ease of understanding and use as defined by the quantified measures that will have been used in the System Specification. It helps testing if the user information can be seen early during development so that any unfriendly features can be "designed out".

*Error exit testing*

At least one test case should be developed to test each system error message and the "satisfactory" error exit of the system upon an error event. For instance, a system should perform a tidy exit, leaving the world in some definite and acceptable state. A good System Specification will have detailed what form this graceful failure will take, particularly in cases where system safety is an issue.

*Help information testing*

Such help information must be sufficient to enable a naïve user to use the system. The System Specification would ideally have quantified how easy it should be for such a user. Tests must be devised to generate help information which must then be evaluated for the appropriate level of detail and presentation. The User Guide must be searched for areas that ought to have help information but where none is available or where help exists but is not documented.

*Limit testing*

At least one test should be developed for each of the documented system limits. Such tests are designed to investigate how the system reacts to data which is maximal or minimal in the sense of attaining some limit specified either in the System Specification or in the User Guide.

During system testing (though not during Acceptance Testing) the system should also be tested beyond the limits specified for it. The purpose here is to find any situations where insufficient safety margins have been built in.

*Stress testing*

Such testing involves running the system under heavy loadings though not necessarily reaching any of the prescribed system limits. For instance, a database system might be stressed with large numbers of database accesses and updates; an air traffic control system might be subjected to a large amount of simulated aircraft traffic; a process control system might be presented with large numbers of sensor interrupts. Stress testing generally requires the use of simulators or traffic generators to push the system being tested in a prescribable and repeatable way.

Stress tests are intended to find errors that only show themselves under certain combinations of events or data values.

Note that since the system will have been built to run within the loading levels defined by the System Specification, tests of its behaviour *outside* this intended envelope cannot form part of the Acceptance Test. They will however be of interest at system testing since knowledge of the system's behaviour beyond the specified call of duty can be useful information.

*Volume testing*

Such tests submit the system to large volumes of data. For instance a large source file with a large number of identifiers for a compiler, a large and complex network for a PERT system, and a large edit for an editor.

Volume testing differs from stress testing in that it seeks to detect errors in function when a large job is being processed. In stress testing one is seeking errors in the system's ability to cope with *instantaneous* peak loadings. Once again, in system testing it is worth pushing the system beyond the levels specified for it in the System Specification so that any inadequate safety margins can be detected.

### Security testing

Tests are performed that attempt to contravene the system's security, such as the access of database-held data by unauthorised users.

### Performance testing

These are tests to probe the system's performance against prescribed timings. Again this will generally require the use of scripted tests that can be timed and repeated. Mechanisms for timing might be necessary, ranging from a stop-watch for coarse measures to oscilloscopes for timings at the millisecond level and below.

### Compatibility testing

Tests are made to probe where the new system does not subsume the facilities and modes of use of the old system where it was intended to do so. In other words a search is made for system incompatibilities. "Upwards compatibility" is generally preferred by users. In data processing systems such tests frequently take the form of *parallel running*. Here the existing system's output is compared with that of the new system; where they are expected to be the same this can be checked. Where the existing system is being enhanced or repaired this is also known as *regression testing*.

### Reliability testing

Specifying *testable* reliability requirements places the greatest test on the writer of the System Specification. Testing those reliability requirements in the short period of the System or Acceptance Test requires imagination on the part of the testers.

Testing for reliability will generally require periods of prolonged use at varying loading levels or possibly constantly at peak level. Reliability levels defined over long periods such as years may need to be interpreted in different ways over a couple of weeks. However, it is highly desirable that reliability tests should take place *in the real environment of the system* wherever possible.

### Recovery testing

This is clearly a vital area of testing for safety critical and similar systems. The system's reaction to failures of all sorts might need to be tested. Situations must be created that create or simulate the types of errors that the system is designed to handle. During the testing, failure conditions should be set up to determine the system's response to them. Responses will have been prescribed for some failure types in the System Specification and they can naturally be checked for. Other failure types will not have a prescribed response in the System Specification and in such cases the actual response will be of concern to the user and designer alike.

### Maintenance potential testing

In some cases a system will be specified to have particular maintenance requirements, for instance that changes of a given level of complexity should take no longer than a given time. Reviews of the design and maintenance documents together with the code are carried out with a view to detecting areas of an incomplete or overly complex nature that could prove difficult to maintain. Maintenance is generally a very expensive business and hence testing before acceptance can generate a substantial long-term saving.

### Installation testing

Here we are concerned with systems that can be installed on a variety of machines or models, or that allow a number of installation options such as different peripheral devices. It is generally impracticable to develop tests for all possible combinations of options when looking for faults in installation mechanisms. However, it is possible to use some of the black-box testing techniques used in module testing once again, exploring maxima and minima and so on. The tester will also want to ensure that the most commonly expected options are tested thoroughly.

### Storage testing

In the case of any system with specified storage requirements such as a maximum amount of main or backing storage occupancy we need to devise tests that seek to detect instances when the system exceeds the specified limits by, for instance, processing or supplying large amounts of data in a similar way to the volume tests.

It is often necessary to develop special *probes* to monitor memory or backing store occupancy and make the necessary measurements.

### Manual procedures testing

Any system that can perform only with manual aid, for instance an archive utility that requires the manual loading of tapes or a system requiring the manual switching of remote devices during processing, will require system tests that concentrate on the manual procedures. The documented procedures in the User Guide are carefully followed in order to detect incompletely specified or even unspecified actions that should be followed. The resilience of the procedure to operator error should also be checked.

### User information testing

The user documents must be reviewed for clarity, ease of use, details of all required system facilities and details of all system error messages together with sufficient information to allow the rectification of errors. The documents must also be reviewed for conformance to any applicable standards. Methods for performing these reviews are detailed in Fagan's paper [Fagan 1976].

# Chapter 5 - The Programmer's View of Testing

## 5.1    Introduction

The programmer's view of the system development life-cycle includes both Module Design and Coding and their counterparts, removing syntax errors and Unit Testing. We can see these activities in the life-cycle fragment in figure 5.1.

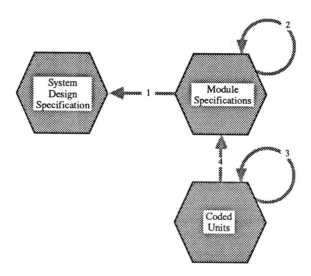

Figure 5.1  -  The programmer's view of the life-cycle

The programmer is presented with portions of the System Design Specification from which they design modules and documents them in Module Specifications. At the same time they should produce a Unit Test Plan which describes how each module (or small group of modules) will be tested as a single unit once it has been coded. The coding stage follows, where Module Specifications are converted (usually manually) into program code.

There are an increasing number of ways in which errors can be detected and removed at compilation time, most of them relying on better tool support. Syntax checking is a form of testing that we naturally expect from our compiler but more is possible. Strongly typed languages such as Ada and Modula-2 effectively prevent the programmer from making mistakes that would otherwise slip through and then have to be discovered by the relatively weak technique of direct testing. Languages such as SPADE-Pascal offer restricted subsets of languages that allow the proof for a given piece of code of various properties such as those detectable by static analysis (qv). Such tools should be considered especially for applications requiring the highest assurances of correctness.

Once a module is in an executable form - a *unit* - it is then tested under the direction of the Unit Test Plan. After satisfactory *unit testing* (where a module, in principle at least, is tested in isolation), modules are released internally under configuration control for *integration testing* as described in chapter 4 - "The Designer's View".

So the programmer produces three main deliverables:

* the Module Specification
* the Unit Test Plan
* module code.

These three must undergo internal quality checks and verification to ensure consistency between themselves and also with the System Design Specification. In the following three sections we treat each of these deliverables in turn and look at some of the methods available for testing them.

## 5.2    Testing the Module Specification

### 5.2.1    Introduction

The Module Specification is the product of module design. Module design takes as its input a software component specification (which is part of the System Design Specification) from which will be produced one or more modules. The aim of module design is to implement the component specification in as reliable a fashion as possible, specifying modules with as many good characteristics as possible, simultaneously reducing the cost of production and maintenance of the software and optimising its performance. (The relative priorities of these design aims should have been stated in the System Design Specification.)

Section 5.2.2 describes methods for testing the *quality* of the Module Specification internally or in relation to other Module Specifications - arrow 2 in figure 5.1. Section 5.2.3 describes its *verification*, ie checking how well it implements the relevant part of the System Design Specification - arrow 1 in figure 5.1.

## 5.2.2   Testing the quality of the Module Specification

This section first describes a number of criteria for evaluating a module design - cohesion, information hiding, coupling, size, complexity and factors affecting testability - and finishes with a discussion of the use of design reviews as the principal technique for testing the quality of Module Specifications against these criteria and the design objectives they define.

*Module design objectives*

There are a number of objectives that we can set for this level of design and they make good criteria against which a design can be tested as well as giving guidelines during the actual design activity. We will be looking for high cohesion, good information hiding, low coupling, modularity, sensible size, and good testability. We now define these qualities.

*- high cohesion*

*Cohesion* is a measure of the relationship between the components of a module and may be thought of as the amount of "glue" that holds the module together. The idea was initially proposed by Stevens, Myers and Constantine [Stevens 1974] and has since been extended by Myers [Myers 1978]. It is not a quantitative measure unfortunately but rather a set of qualitative levels. The seven levels (ranked from least desirable to most desirable) are listed in the following table.

---

*The levels of cohesion*

*Coincidental*:   there is no significant relationship between the components of a module, ie they are only together by coincidence.

*Logical*:   the module performs one set of logically related functions, eg a number of Print Routines combined within a single module - no data is passed and none of them work together, they merely perform the logically related function of printing.

*Temporal*:   elements are related in time, eg the separate operations of an initialisation routine.

*Procedural*: the processing elements of a module are related and must be executed in a specific order.

*Communicational*: functions operating on common data are grouped together.

*Sequential*: the module represents a portion of a data flow, ie it accepts data, transforms it, and passes it on.

*Functional*: every process within a module contributes directly to performing one single function.

---

*- good information hiding*

Information hiding is related to cohesion (otherwise known as *informational strength*), and in the cohesion scale given above it falls somewhere between sequential and functional cohesion. Information hiding as a design principle favours the production of highly independent modules. Design decisions internal to a module are hidden and do not affect the correctness of its co-operation with other modules.

A module with informational strength performs a number of functions where the functions (represented by entry points in the module) deal with a single data structure. Thus, users of the module (ie other modules) may access, through function calls alone, the information the module "protects". The information cannot be accessed by direct manipulation of the module's private data, or by the use of global variables.

There is an apparent contradiction here. Informational strength may be regarded as an improvement over functional strength but it is below it on the scale. The reason for this is that it is harder to deal with and the chance of error is greater. The resultant module can easily have all the disadvantages of logical strength unless great care is taken to make sure that the coding of each function is independent of the other functions in the module.

*- low coupling*

*Coupling* is the degree of connection between modules. It should be minimised. The three types of coupling (again in order of increasing desirability) are defined in the following table.

*The levels of coupling*

> *High coupling* (also termed *external, content* or *pathological* ): one module refers to the internal contents of another module. This occurs if a problem is partitioned in an arbitrary way.

> *Control coupling*: one module passes a conditional flag to another where the operation of the recipient is dependent upon the value of the flag.

> *Data coupling*: one module passes data to another as part of an invocation or return of control; the fewer pieces of data passed, the better the design can withstand change.

It should be noted that whilst these concepts of cohesion and coupling might be valuable when evaluating a module or choosing a decomposition into modules, they do not provide a method of attaining these levels. However, object-oriented design starts with the premise that data coupling in particular should be promoted.

*- modularity*

A great deal of literature extols the benefits of "modularity", but very little is said about how to achieve it. A major difference between good and poor program structures concerns their complexity and there are three universal means of reducing complexity in any system, namely *partitioning, representation as hierarchy* and *maximising independence*.

The maximising of module independence is a useful aim when deciding a program's structure. As we have seen, useful measures of module independence are module cohesion (which is determined by analysing the functions of the module) and module coupling (which is determined by analysing the data that are jointly referenced by the two modules and the methods used to share that data). The overall design goal is to maximise cohesion and to minimise coupling.

No claim is made that module strength and coupling completely define the independence of modules. They do, however, define the general conditions of independence.

*Reducing system complexity*

> *Partitioning*: reduces the number of factors a designer's mind has to keep track of simultaneously in order to comprehend the program; it creates a number of well-defined, documented boundaries (ie interfaces which show us which data items are relevant to a particular piece of program code etc).

> *Hierarchy*: allows us to separate our ideas iteratively and to deal with increasing amounts of detail; different levels of design describe the system at different levels of abstraction.

> *Independence*: determines how to partition a program into a hierarchical structure such that each module is as independent as possible of other modules.

*- module size*

Module size is really a secondary guideline contributing to a well-designed program structure. "Good" module size is difficult to define and it tends to be language-dependent. If a program contains too many small modules, anyone attempting to understand the program will have too many pieces to juggle mentally. A program with too many large modules has the problems associated with insufficient partitioning: too few well-defined interfaces and too many simultaneous thoughts required by the designer or maintainer. Tradition has it that one or two pages of code make a module that will fit in a person's mind.

*- good testability*

Increasing modularity is often thought to decrease the testing problem as in the following example.

If Module A is made up of two blocks of code X and Y which handle 10 and 8 special cases respectively, then the number of paths through this module would be potentially 80 (=10 x 8). Reformatting A into two modules B and C with low coupling would mean there would be 18 (=10 + 8) paths. However, the number of paths through even a small module is so astronomical that a comprehensive testing plan is out of the question. It is more realistic to maximise a testing coverage measure (see section 5.3.4) which demands a level of effort which increases in approximate proportion to the size of the module. Therefore the effort required to achieve the same testing coverage with the smaller modules is not significantly different from that with the large module from which they were derived.

## Design reviews

*Reviews* - alias *walkthroughs* or *inspections* - carried out on the design of a module aim to remove errors before code is written.

The inspection process works best when the participants play particular roles. When code is reviewed there is typically the presenter of the item under review, a moderator, the prospective coder/implementer and the tester. These roles are described in detail in [Fagan 1976]. The time taken to do inspections and any resulting rework must be scheduled and managed with the same attention as other important project activities. Fagan also emphasises the importance of a single objective: the objective of an inspection is to detect errors, not to correct them. No attempt should be made to redesign, or evaluate alternative design solutions; all effort should be put into finding errors. Perhaps the most important element of reviews is that they should be conducted in an egoless fashion - it is the product that is being reviewed and not the producer.

Reviews do have a number of drawbacks: even though they are effective in terms of finding errors they tend to be expensive, motivation of personnel may be difficult after a short period of time, and it may take several sessions to complete one program.

Fagan's approach to inspections can be summarised as follows:

1    Describe the program development in terms of operations, and define exit criteria which must be satisfied for completion of each operation.
2    Separate the objectives of the inspection process to keep the inspection team focused on one objective at a time.
3    Classify detected errors by type, and rank by frequency of occurrence of types. Identify which types to spend most time looking for in the inspection.
4    Describe how to look for the presence of error types.
5    Analyse inspection results and use them for constant process improvement (once process averages have been reached they can be used for control of the process).

One of the objectives of a Module Specification review is to ensure that module independence in the program has been raised as much as possible. The reviewers should look for implicit or explicit assumptions and dependencies among modules, and then consider eliminating these dependencies through the appropriate application of informational strength modules or by carrying out further design or decomposition.

A static design review should also take place and may employ an independent observer to ask key questions. The whole purpose of the review should be to find weaknesses in the design and not to attempt to make immediate improvements.

The following table contains some of the points to look for in a design.

---

*Design review checklist*

Does the module have functional or informational strength? If not, why not?

Is each pair of modules either data-coupled or not directly coupled (no direct coupling being the lowest interaction possible)? If not, why not?

Is the decomposition complete, ie can the logic of each module be visualised?

Is there any unnecessary redundancy in the interface?

Are the interface data to each module consistent with the definition of the module's function?

Are there modules in the program that seem to perform the same function?

Is each module described by its function (what the module does) rather than by its context (a particular usage of the module) or logic (how the module performs its function)? Has each function been stated accurately?

Are there any pre-existing modules that could have been used in the program?

Are there any restrictive modules (ie modules that are over-specialised)?

Are the modules predictable? (A *predictable* module is one whose function remains constant from one call to another, ie it has no memory. A module that alters a local variable to retain a value between invocations could be unpredictable.)

Is there any aspect of the design that is precluded by the programming language to be used or by local standards?

Is the hierarchical structure too extreme (eg "short and fat" or "tall and lean")?

Does the design contain anything that might be easily misunderstood?

Have any unstated assumptions been made?

---

Documentation is important, not only for the purpose of maintenance, but also as a post-design check. To allow such checking we can expect to provide a minimum of information provided for each module along the lines of the following table. Formal specifications such as those produced by using formal methods like VDM and Z are ideal.

---

*Module documentation*

> *Module name*: a definition of the name that is used (eg in a CALL statement) to reference the module. It should be descriptive of the function performed by the module.
>
> *Function*: described in a single sentence followed by an expanded description (if necessary). Only the function (not the internal logic) should be described here.
>
> *Inputs*: a precise description of all input data to the module (all input parameters, order, size, type and range of values). If the module is more than data-coupled then input descriptions will be more complex.
>
> *Outputs*: a precise description of all output data from the module (output parameters, physical order, size, type, range and error information, eg return codes). If different classes of outputs may be returned then the outputs should be described in terms of cause and effect relationships with input.
>
> *External effects*: actions that manifest themselves outside the program (eg reading a tape) should be documented as part of the module external specification.

---

## 5.2.3 Verification of the Module Specification

Here we are interested in the verification of the Module Specification against part of the System Design Specification. The aim is to check that the Module Design fulfils the requirements expressed in the System Design Specification. This again will generally be the subject of reviews which are the principal method of verification outside of the formal methods that are now emerging from research. Of these it is worth mentioning again VDM [Jones 1980] [Jones 1986] which offers a formal technique for specifying a module in terms of *preconditions* and *postconditions* expressed in terms of the data on which the module acts. The method allows such a specification to be successfully refined and for each refinement to be verified (tested) against the higher level one. The method also allows an implementation in the form of a particular algorithm to be verified as being a correct implementation of the specification.

If reviews are being used, the questions to be asked are:

- have all the functions in the System Design Specification been carried forward into the Module Specification?
- does the module do more than what is required by the System Design Specification?
- does the Module Specification correctly refine the higher level specification in the System Design Specification?

## 5.3 Testing the Unit Test Plan

### 5.3.1 Introduction

At the same time as the Module Specification is being produced, a Testing Plan for the ensuing coded module should be written. A major amount of testing (ie that of all the individual coded units) will depend on this plan so it is important that it is itself subject to quality and verification tests.

Section 5.3.2 deals with tests on the internal quality of the Unit Test Plan. Sections 5.3.3 and 5.3.4 treat the verification of the Unit Test Plan against the System Design Specification (*requirements-directed testing*) and against the Module Specification (*design-directed testing*) respectively.

### 5.3.2 Checking the quality of the Unit Test Plan

The Unit Test Plan must be checked to ensure that it follows whatever standards are laid down, for instance the specification of the test drivers and stubs to be used, the input test data and the expected results. Here is another subject for review with the character of quality assurance. Review methods are described in section 5.2.

### 5.3.3 Requirements-directed generation of test data

The choice of suitable test data should be based first of all on the *functional* requirements of the module as expressed in the System Design Specification, ie by treating it as a "black-box". *Black-box* techniques are important as it is essential that the module performs all the functions required of it. This importance is even greater when modelling or prototyping techniques are being employed in the life-cycle. In this section we outline some of the basic techniques of black-box testing. Although these topics have been mentioned in earlier chapters we cover them again this time from the perspective of testing software modules. For a detailed description of the methods see [Myers 1979] and [Beizer 1983]. For an example of black-box testing based on a *formal specification* see [Hayes 1986]. Here, the specification language Z is used to give a precise specification for a program or module; during the development process, information generated about (for instance) the relationship between the specification and the implementation is used to steer the testing of the resulting code.

### *Equivalence partitioning*

This technique relies on looking at the set of valid inputs specified for the module - its *domain* - and dividing it up into classes of data that should, according to the specification, be treated identically. These *equivalence classes* will not overlap and one set of test data is then chosen to represent each equivalence class. The premise is that any representative will be as good as any other in the same class at finding errors in the handling of that class.

### *Boundary-value analysis*

This complements equivalence partitioning by looking at a fruitful source of errors: the boundaries of the input equivalence classes. Test cases are devised that exercise the module with data chosen from these boundaries and also with data chosen to exercise the module on the boundaries of output data as well. For instance, if a module does one thing for $x<0$ and something else for $x \geq 0$ it should be tested with $x=0$ as well as $x=-100$ and $x=+100$, two test values that equivalence partitioning might suggest.

### *Cause-effect graphing*

Equivalence partitioning and boundary-value analysis exercise the module by looking at each equivalence class in isolation. But they do not exercise the module with different combinations of inputs from the equivalence classes. *Cause-effect graphing* is a way of doing this whilst avoiding the major combinatorial problems that can arise. The technique uses diagrams that are easy on small problems but quickly become unmanageable as the problem size increases. The end result is a decision table that can then be turned into test data sets by the techniques of equivalence partitioning and boundary values.

*Error guessing*

More a form of cynicism than a technique, error guessing relies on the instincts of the tester to look for those inputs that are "likely" to cause a program to fail: variables set to zero, lists empty, tables full, duplicated names, etc. This should be the last technique used to generate test cases, to "top up" the test cases derived systematically by other means. Unfortunately, it is often the only test data selection technique used. Error guessing is best done with a comprehensive checklist similar to that in section 5.4.2. If you continuously update your own version of this checklist then it becomes a very powerful technique as it focuses on the weaknesses of the individual programmer or designer involved. It also becomes firmly related to the type of work done in your organisation.

## 5.3.4   Design-directed generation of test data

At first sight it might appear enough to rely on black-box testing - after all, that tests a module against what it is supposed to do. Unfortunately, black-box techniques make the unjustified assumption that the structure of the input space says something about the structure of the module and hence the errors in it. Indeed, it is claimed that even "good" black-box testing will only exercise 50% to 70% of the code. In other words 30% to 50% of the code could remain untested!

To make sure that the module is "fully" exercised to some level, we therefore need to supplement black-box testing by choosing further test cases that take into account the internal structure or design of the module to be tested. This is the purpose of *white-box* techniques. Note that we cannot use just white-box testing because we could not be certain of having tested whether the module had the right functionality.

The ideal situation would be to exercise every entry-to-exit path in the module but often this is combinatorially prohibitive so we may have to settle for a lesser goal. In order to see how close a particular level of testing is to the ideal we need to have *coverage measures*. These measure the proportion of a module that has been tested by a given set of test cases. A corresponding *coverage criterion* gives us guidance on choosing test cases to yield a high (perhaps 100%) coverage for that measure. There are a number of different ways of defining *coverage*. They vary in the "segments" into which they divide the code forming a module. We will look at three different criteria and their corresponding measures.

*Statement coverage*

The *statement coverage criterion* is that each statement in the module is executed at least once. This would seem to be really comprehensive. However, in fact it can omit important cases.

99

Consider the following **If** statement (we use a structured language of the Pascal variety for illustrative purposes):

**If (X>0) or (Y=2) then A := A+X**

We could test this single statement with a single test case that ensured that either X>0 or that Y=2. The assignment to A would then be carried out. In doing this we would satisfy the simple statement coverage criterion. However we do also need to check the situation in which the assignment is *not* carried out: perhaps the **or** is in error and should have been an **and** or perhaps the statement should have said X>1. So we need further test cases to exercise the other outcome of the conditional expression (X>0) **or** (Y=2). There are in fact a number of levels of coverage that can be defined, going up to one requiring test cases that exercise every combination of every outcome of every component in every complex conditional expression. The level of coverage chosen for a particular module must be determined by its "criticality".

### Testing with reference to a flow graph

A *flow graph* is similar in some respects to a flow chart and is used to represent the flow of control from one statement to another in a module. Such a graph consists of a number of *nodes* connected in pairs by *arcs* or *edges*. There must be only one entry node but there may be several exit nodes. The nodes represent actions and tests in the module and the arcs represent transfer of control. Since high-level languages have structured statements, identification of the nodes to statements is not straightforward, because flow of control exists within such statements. In order to bring out this flow of control and thus construct the flow graph, it is useful to imagine the reduction of these structured statements (in Pascal they are **If**, **while**, **repeat**, **for**, **case** and in other languages would include jumps arising from exceptions) to merely conditional and unconditional jumps.

For example, the statement in Pascal:

**If X<>0 then Y := Y+X else Z := Y;**

becomes conceptually (for the purposes of constructing the flow graph)

```
      If X=0 then goto 1;
      Y := Y+ X;
      goto 2;
1:    Z: = Y;
2:    ...
```

It is necessary to consider a module in this way in order to construct a flow graph. Once the rules for decomposing the various structured statements are understood, a flow graph can be constructed from structured code. Figure 5.2 illustrates flow graph representations of three Pascal structures. An unshaded node represents a statement following the structure depicted.

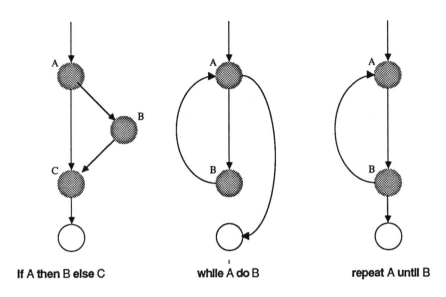

If A then B else C          while A do B          repeat A until B

Figure 5.2 - Flow graphs of three Pascal constructs

A node in the flow graph could represent one statement in this unstructured code, but it is better to make a single node by combining a sequence of statements from which it is not possible to jump into or out of except at the start and end. This is termed a *basic block*. If any statement in a basic block is executed, then every statement in it is executed in the given sequence. A coverage criterion based on basic blocks will not be an improvement over statement coverage. However, coverage of *arcs* will overcome the deficiency mentioned above.

If enough test cases are written to cover all arcs in a flow graph, this is called *decision coverage*.

If a decision is complex (eg I<LAST **and** P=Q) then merely testing for an overall **true** or **false** result may miss some errors. The *condition coverage criterion* stipulates that both **true** and **false** outcomes must be generated for each component of a complex condition. Both outcomes of the overall decision must also be tested, of course.

*Linear code sequence and jump (LCSAJ)*

Another method of segmenting module code is in terms of LCSAJs. An LCSAJ can best be understood in terms of the unstructured form of code described above (although some of the labels referred to below may not be explicitly written by the programmer). An LCSAJ is a sub-path through part of the flow graph whose start point is either the first line of the program, or a labelled statement (ie it is the target line of a jump), and whose end point is either an unconditional **goto**, or a conditional **goto** with the condition evaluated to **true**.

Several LCSAJs may overlap for one of the following two reasons:

- non-redundant labels may occur in a sequence of non-jumping statements
- conditional **goto**s may occur in the middle of an LCSAJ in the situation where the condition evaluates to **false**.

Overlapping LCSAJs represent different test cases differing in their test data, within a small part of the module. Each basic block is also an LCSAJ, but certain sequences of two or more basic blocks may also be LCSAJs. LCSAJs represent somewhat larger units than basic blocks. Typically an LCSAJ is four times as long as a basic block. Research results have shown that LCSAJ coverage criteria are more effective at finding errors than decision coverage criteria [Woodward 1980].

*Dynamic data flow analysis*

All the testing coverage criteria described so far are based on the flow of *control*. This measure examines the effect of basic blocks upon *data* items. One block may set up a value, another may reference it. The data flow coverage criterion takes basic blocks in pairs with respect to each data item where the first member of each pair sets up the data item and the second member references it. The criterion is satisfied when each dependent pair is exercised. See [Rapps 1985].

Extensive computation may be required to calculate the coverage. In a module with $n$ basic blocks then for each data item there are $n(n-1)/2$ possible pairs although in practice only a proportion will have dependencies.

*Revealing subdomains*

Finally we mention a technique which combines white-box and black-box techniques through the use of so-called *revealing subdomains* [Weyuker 1980]. We have seen how we can divide the input domain of the module into equivalence classes of data that *should* be treated in the same way by analysing the specification of the module. We can also, by examination of the code and symbolic evaluation (qv), divide up the input domain into classes of data that *are* treated in the same way. By taking the intersection of these two domains we obtain a number of subdomains of data from which we then select our test data. Techniques for choosing the data in such a way that errors are most likely to be revealed are discussed in [Weyuker 1980].

## 5.4     Unit testing

### 5.4.1     Introduction

When a module has been coded from its module specification and all errors detectable by a compiler have been removed, it is ready to undergo *unit testing*. Such testing can as usual be divided into two categories. The first is that consisting of quality checks - examining the code using external general criteria and standards to evaluate its good (and bad) characteristics. These are dealt with in section 5.4.2 below. The second category is that of verification of coded units, evaluating the modules against the Module Specification using the Unit Test Plan and this is covered in section 5.4.3. The final section, 5.4.4, covers other techniques used to support the testing process.

### 5.4.2     Checking the quality of coded units

#### Dry running

This method of reviewing modules is normally performed by the programmer of the module before submitting the code to a group review. It consists of mentally executing the code with example test cases, noting the values of variables as they are changed and the path through the program. This has the advantage that as the programmer goes through the code they can consider whether the path taken is always the one intended and can ensure that the values of the variables are always sensible. The programmer is best qualified to do this as they have the best understanding of the program and knows the intended function of each part.

#### Structured walkthroughs

In the context of module testing, a *structured walkthrough* is a review of a program module carried out by a meeting of a group of people selected from the development project. The meeting is planned by the originator of the module or a senior programmer, or, in the case of testing teams, this may be done by the team coordinator. The originator of the module explains the module design using a formal agenda to the participants who point out defects and discuss issues relating to the module in an effort to identify errors. The originator of the module is responsible for correcting the defects found. The repairs should be reviewed in a later walkthrough.

### Fagan Inspections

Like all reviewing methods, *Fagan Inspections* [Fagan 1976] are used to minimise the cost of correcting errors by attempting to find them as early as possible. They are therefore to be used during module design as well as coding.

Inspections in this phase of the life-cycle are prescribed at the point where a clean compilation has been obtained. Unlike a design inspection, no time need be spent in describing the overall area and how the module fits into it, since the participants should already be familiar with it. This greatly reduces the time for review and increases its effectiveness since the "difficult" areas are inspected first.

Checklists of error types and key questions for individual scrutiny will be different for coding from those for design. Checklists will again vary with programming language and the type of system being built (eg real-time, communications and commercial). Some example checklists for commercial systems are provided below. The first is a checklist for the requirements placed upon modules, sub-programs and programs. It could also apply to the execution of code.

---

### Module requirements checklist

Job control functions have no errors.
File conditions are correct for predicted volumes and growth.
Execution time and program size are within tolerance.
Input data is accepted correctly.
All error or progress messages are shown to be produced correctly.
Program termination is correct, in normal and abnormal situations.
Missing or empty files are handled correctly.
Parameter passing or condition code returns are correct.
Specific combinations of input records are shown to be accepted.
Control totals are correct.
Output field sizes are correct and adequate.
Reports have been checked for spelling, layout, and page numbers.
Rounding errors have been eliminated or accounted for.
Control breaks have been demonstrated.
Updating of master files has been checked.
The handling of first and last records has been checked.
Double updates are absent.

---

In the next checklist we look at some common coding errors that can be checked for at inspections.

*Some common coding errors*

Poor or non-standard style.
Omission in coding of logic element.
Wrong use of subscripts or indices.
Improper address modification.
Reference to undefined symbols.
Multiply defined symbols or data names.
Transcription of the characters in a name.
Wrong initialisation of fields, counters, flags.
Incorrect or missing saving and restoration of registers.
Use of absolute addresses.
Incorrect format of statements.
Uncleared buffers, print lines, registers.
Incorrect calling of subroutines.
Incorrect setting of parameters or switches.
Creation of endless loops.
Overwriting of constants.
Failure to allow for overflow.
Wrong branches of logic.
Poor organisation of **If** or **case** constructions.
Improper termination of loops.
Wrong number of loop cycles.
Loop initialisation incorrect.
Failure to open or close files.
Failure to manage print lines correctly.
Poor cohesion of the logic.
Poor coupling of the logic modules.
Incorrect linkage to the operating system.
Wrongly set variables.
Use of alias or re-use of variables.
Poor comments; not enough *why* or *when*.

*Static analysis*

Static analysis of source code gathers global information concerning the structure of a module or a set of modules in order to find anomalies. There are three kinds of analysis: *control flow analysis, data flow analysis* and *information flow analysis*. Tool sets for the automatic static analysis of code are becoming increasingly available though they are generally language-specific; for instance, SPADE operates on a subset of Pascal designed to prevent errors that could not be detected by static analysis.

*- control flow analysis*

Control flow analysis builds up a control flow graph as described in section 5.3.4. This graph can then be analysed for anomalies, which include:

- multiple entries
- multiple exits
- unreachable code
- loops with multiple entries
- non-conformance to structured programming standards (although, unless extensions are allowed, constructions like *quits* in Jackson-style designs will be incorrectly flagged).

*- data flow analysis*

This analysis builds on the flow graph obtained above to study each variable in the module to determine where it is defined, undefined (ie disappears from scope) and used on all paths through the program. For example, this kind of analysis can detect that a particular variable is uninitialised on some possible control paths through a program or that a variable is assigned a value which is never used on any subsequent path through the program.

The anomalies discovered by data flow analysis are often symptomatic of misspellings, confusion of names and omission of statements.

This kind of analysis provides a very comprehensive coverage of all paths through a program which actual execution could never achieve, since in general the number of different control paths through a program is astronomical. The weakness of this analysis, however, is that it cannot distinguish infeasible paths through the program from feasible ones. An *infeasible path* is one which can never be achieved in actual execution because, for example, a pair of conditions on that path are mutually exclusive: because of the logic of the program they can never both be true. Furthermore, it can be proved mathematically that, however sophisticated the analyser, it is impossible in general to identify such paths algorithmically, eg with a computer program.

### - information flow analysis

This relatively new technique is derived from investigations into the security of computer systems. It determines the influences, direct or indirect, among the input data values, the computation of expressions, and the output data values. Such analysis can in some cases reveal:

- statements that can use undefined variables
- ineffective statements, whose execution cannot affect the final value of any exported variable
- incorrect usage of input variables
- loops that will not terminate.

It has the same drawbacks as data flow analysis but within these limitations static analysers can provide information over and above that normally obtained by a compiler, including information about:

- subprograms called by each subprogram
- uninitialised variables
- variables that are set but never used
- unreachable segments of code
- misuse of shared variables
- mismatch of parameter lists (by numbers, type or use)
- departures from coding standards.

Static analysis may be considered complementary to actual test execution: it should be performed prior to dynamic testing. The results should be examined critically: not all anomalies are necessarily coding mistakes.

### Symbolic execution

*Symbolic execution* represents a mid-point between running individual test sets through a program and carrying out a proof of its correctness.

It involves executing (interpreting) a program symbolically. During symbolic execution, the values of variables are held in algebraic form. Thus, suppose that on entry to the following program the parameters I and J have values $I$ and $J$ respectively:

```
Integer procedure P (Integer I, J);
begin
        Integer L1, L1;
        L1 := (I + J)/2;
        L2 := (G**2 + L1) * J;
        return (L1 + L2)/2;
end P
```

Then if $G$ is the value of global G on entry to P, the value returned by P will be:

$$((I + J)/2 + (G**2 + (I + J)/2) *J )/2$$

Programs with decisions are clearly more complex to handle. Unless the value of a condition at a decision can be proved to be always **true** or **false** from the symbolic values of the variables at the point of the decision, it is necessary to follow both outcomes whilst remembering their respective condition values. It is this fact that makes symbolic execution very cumbersome for most commercial programs, especially on-line programs in which the values of input data often govern the path taken during execution.

At the end of the evaluation, there will be two facts about each path through the program: a list of the decision outcomes along the path and the final values of all the variables expressed algebraically. Together these define the function of the program and can be compared with the required function - this is the test. (In practice many paths will be infeasible and will have to be pruned out if combinatorial explosions are to be avoided.)

Loops require more work to analyse them successfully. It might be necessary to determine the algebraic outcome of a loop by induction. And there is a further problem when symbolically executing programs in which array element access (ie via array subscripts) is dependent on the values of the module's inputs. Techniques similar to program proving must be used in these cases, but this is outside the scope of this book. (See [Clarke 1981] and [Clarke 1985].)

Symbolic evaluation can be of value for arithmetic expressions such as payroll calculations and invoice calculations, but can be cumbersome if done manually and may only be worth the effort for a system with stringent reliability requirements.

The technique of *partition analysis* [Richardson 1985] combines the two techniques of symbolic execution and equivalence partitioning to give a verification method and a method for generating test cases. Equivalence partitioning is used to derive *functional subdomains* and symbolic execution (or in this case *evaluation*) to derive *implementation subdomains*. By forming the intersection of these subdomains we arrive at a partition of the input space that provides a basis for choosing test cases as in the simple equivalence partitioning technique.

## 5.4.3    Verification of coded units

*Verification against the Module Specification*

Direct verification of the code against the specification, as distinct from verification via the Unit Test Plan, is rare.  Apart from the ubiquitous review, one method is to use a structure chart generator.  This program processes the module source file or a compiler listing and generates a structure chart reflecting the actual structure of the code.  This can be compared with the Module Specification.  Structure chart generators are many and various but often depend on comments in the source text which may not actually bear a correct relationship to the code.  Plainly structure chart generators which are able to process the programming language syntax to some extent are preferable.

*Verification against the Unit Test Plan*

This activity is what is sometimes naïvely considered to be the whole of testing:  executing a module with test data and examining the result.  We have already discussed methods of choosing test data - see sections 5.3.3. and 5.3.4.  We now go on to describe ways of carrying out testing.

*- test harnesses*

There are two strategies for testing modules by actual execution: top-down and bottom-up.  Either one or a combination of these two approaches can be used.

In the *top-down* approach, the top-level subprogram is tested, with the lower-level subprograms being substituted by dummy or null routines called *stubs*.  Stubs should be set to always return one of their eventually required values, eg a stub validate module might be set to return the condition **valid** for all transactions.  In more sophisticated stubs there might be a switch on test case number to provide the return condition required for that test case.  Later, of course, the stub will have the code necessary for it to return a correct response.  A test harness may be used to call the top-level subprogram.  As testing progresses the stubs are replaced by the real routines which at first call more stubs representing lower levels in the module hierarchy.  In this way, each module is provided naturally with an environment (very largely its final one) in which it can be tested.  Unfortunately, it is often very difficult to arrange things so that all possible desired inputs for thorough testing can be applied to the module under test.

The *bottom-up* approach avoids this difficulty by constructing a special test harness which directly calls the module under test, which may call other modules already tested.  This has the advantage of allowing the tester to have complete control over the test data, but at the expense of having to write extra code. In fact, errors discovered can prove to be in the test harness! Specially written test harnesses deserve to be produced as rigorously as the application code proper, including subjection to configuration control.

Generalised test harnesses exist for specific languages and operating systems. Even so, such harnesses may still require a small, specially written interface routine. Ideally such harnesses should be written in the same language as the module under test.

A test harness reads test data from a file, passes it to the module under test and records the resulting output. The harness may also provide a facility for recording snapshots of data areas that the module is updating. Another facility is the verification of test results by comparing the actual results with values predicted from the functions of the module under test and reporting any discrepancies. Again such verification is often applied as much to the predicted values as the module under test! Nevertheless correcting such test results files is valuable because of their later use in regression testing during maintenance. Test harnesses that operate in batch mode provide an automatic means of carrying out tests.

A test harness may also provide the stubs required in top-down testing. These stubs may cause the parameters passed to them to be recorded and obtain values to be returned from the test data source file.

### - random testing

In this method, an automatic test driver generates a large number of random inputs from the set of valid values specified for the module. The module is executed for each of these inputs and the results printed together with the input values. The results are then checked manually. Experimental results from using this method on systems [Panzl 1978] have shown that significantly fewer errors remain undetected than with "conventional testing" where the tester chooses the test cases. The method has been much used, for instance by IBM Federal Systems Division, on large systems of modules in conjunction with error-guessing by human testers and has proved successful in this combination. For single modules, however, it is unclear whether the results would be so good if the Unit Test Plan had been produced and verified as we described above. Random testing may however be an alternative to using these methods, requiring less mental effort. Checking the results would seem to be lengthy and tedious without automatic assistance.

### - dual programming

Verification of a code unit can also be performed with respect to *another version* of the same unit programmed independently from an independently produced Module Specification by the use of a *dual automatic test driver* [Panzl 1978]. Such a

110

test driver is similar to the sort of test harness discussed above except that it executes both versions of the unit with the same randomly produced test data. The results are then compared automatically. If they agree the test case is discarded. Only if the outputs differ in some way are the inputs and outputs printed. The cause of the disagreement is then investigated. Two possibilities exist: either one of the programmers has made a mistake in either the Module Specification or the module, or there is an ambiguity in the System Design Specification, which must be resolved. Results of experiments in using this method, which compensate for the differing abilities of individual programmers, demonstrate an order of magnitude improvement over "conventional testing" (with the same reservations as above). The method has the additional advantage of more verification of the System Design Specification, but the cost of module design and coding is doubled.

## 5.4.4 Supporting techniques

So far in this chapter we have discussed testing methods that are based on the analysis of the program text and upon the actual execution of the code. This final section deals with some techniques to support these methods.

*Fault diagnosis*

When testing has revealed a fault it is often difficult to diagnose its cause. If the cause is not apparent perhaps after careful dry-running of the test data then techniques must be used to obtain more information on events associated with the fault. This, therefore, inevitably means doing further tests perhaps monitoring such information as the value of certain data items and the course of program execution. Reproducibility of the test is essential. It may, however, be sufficient to design more test data to determine the location of the error.

*Evaluation of test effectiveness*

An independent assessment of the effectiveness of module testing is a desirable feature of quality control. Techniques to measure the quality of the test data will provide an indication of testing effectiveness but cannot provide a reliable estimate of number of errors remaining.

Testing coverage measures examine the number of execution paths resulting from the testing exercise. They have already been discussed in section 5.3.4.

*Mutation analysis* is a technique of deliberately seeding further errors into a tested module and then re-running the tests to see how many of such known errors can be detected. The proportion of errors so found provides another measure of testing effectiveness. It is, however, rather laborious and can give rise to many time-consuming runs due to system aborts and infinite loops. Once again, automatic assistance is called for.

### Quality Assurance

*Quality Assurance* is usually performed internally on a development project by an examination of program code, possibly by a member of project management, to ensure a high and uniform standard. The main purpose of this is to provide a product that is easy to maintain, something that is only possible if the program text is readable, easy to understand and not idiosyncratic. To this end, project standards concerning, for example, commenting conventions for descriptive information about each module, naming conventions, the size of modules, and (perhaps) restrictions in the use of certain language features, must be set up at the start of the project. Quality audits will then check for adherence to these standards. Static analyses can also be used to provide an automated form of quality assurance.

Complexity measures, such as McCabe's *cyclomatic number* [McCabe 1976], can also be used if a suitable tool is available, but some research has suggested that the number of lines of code is at least as good a measure of complexity as any other proposed metric.

### Error analysis

Development project control can be improved by the collection and storage of error data, ideally with a good classification of errors. Analysis can monitor the progress of testing and reveal omissions. By examining the number of errors found per hundred lines of code for different modules, anomalies are pinpointed. If the error density is low, this may indicate inadequate testing or a very simple structure. If it is too high the module concerned should be investigated and it might even indicate the necessity for redesign.

In another method the errors are plotted against time for each module. It has been noted that a small proportion, about 20%, of any system being developed tends to contain the majority of the defects. Error analysis should identify these 20% modules and the information used to concentrate efforts. This is particularly important towards the end of a project phase if time begins to run out and the time available for more comprehensive testing decreases.

# Bibliography

[Alford 1980] Alford, M. W. (1980). Software Requirements Engineering Methodology (SREM) at the age of four. In *Proceedings of the International Computer Software and Applications Conference*, pp866-874. New York: IEEE Computer Society Press.

[Ambler 1977] Ambler, A. L. *et al.* (1977). *Gypsy: a language for specification and implementation of verifiable programs.* SIGPLAN Notices, **12**, 3, 1-10.

[Beizer 1983] Beizer, B. (1983). *Software testing techniques.* New York: Van Nostrand Reinhold.

[Beizer 1984] Beizer, B. (1984). *Software system testing techniques and quality assurance.* New York: Van Nostrand Reinhold.

[Bersoff 1981] Bersoff, E. H., Henderson, V. D., & Siegel, S. G. (1981). *Software configuration management. An investment in product integrity.* Englewood Cliffs, N.J.: Prentice-Hall.

[Birrell 1985] Birrell, N. D., & Ould, M. A. (1985). *A practical handbook for software development.* Cambridge, England: Cambridge University Press.

[Boehm 1981] Boehm, B. W. (1981). *Software Engineering Economics.* Englewood Cliffs, N.J.: Prentice-Hall.

[Booch 1986] Booch, G. (1986). Object oriented development. *IEEE Transactions on Software Engineering*, **SE-12**, 2, 211-221.

[Brooks 1975] Brooks, F. P. (1975). *The Mythical Man-Month.* Reading, Mass.: Addison-Wesley.

[Bruno 1986] Bruno, G., & Marchetto, G. (1986). Process-translatable Petri nets for the rapid prototyping of process control systems. *IEEE Transactions on Software Engineering*, **SE-12**, 2, 346-357.

[Clarke 1981] Clarke, L. A., & Richardson, D. J. (1981). Symbolic evaluation methods - implementation and applications. In *Computer program testing*, eds B. Chandrasekaran & S. Radicchi. Amsterdam: North-Holland.

[Clarke 1985]     Clarke, L. A., & Richardson, D. J. (1985). Applications of symbolic evaluation. *Journal of Systems and Software*, 5, 1, 15-35

[Cohen 1986]      Cohen, B., Harwood, W., & Jackson, M. I. (1986). *The specification of complex systems*. Reading, Mass: Addison-Wesley.

[Dickinson 1980]  Dickinson, B. (1980). *Developing structured systems*. New York: Yourdon Press.

[Fagan 1976]      Fagan, M. E. (1976). Design and code inspections to reduce errors in program development. *IBM Systems Journal*, 15, 182-211.

[Freedman 1979]   Freedman, D. P., & Weinberg, G. M. (1979). *Ethnotechnical Review Handbook*. Lincoln, Nebraska, USA: Ethnotech Inc.

[Gane 1979]       Gane, C., & Sarson, T. (1979). *Structured systems analysis: tools and techniques*. Englewood Cliffs, N.J.: Prentice-Hall.

[Gilb 1986]       Gilb, T. (1986). Tools for "Design by Objectives". In *Software: Requirements, Specification and Testing*. Oxford: Blackwell Scientific Publications.

[Gowers 1986]     Gowers, E. (1986). *The Complete Plain Words*. London: Her Majesty's Stationery Office.

[Greenspan 1984]  Greenspan, S. J. (1984). *Requirements modeling: a knowledge representation approach to software requirements definition*. Technical Report CSRG-155, Computer Systems Research Group, University of Toronto.

[Hayes 1986]      Hayes, I. J. (1986). Specification directed module testing. *IEEE Transactions on Software Engineering*, SE-12, 1, 124-133.

[Henderson 1985]  Henderson, P., & Minkowitz, C. (1985). *The me too method of software design*. Report FPN/10, Department of Computer Science, University of Stirling, UK.

[Henderson 1986]  Henderson, P. (1986). Functional programming, formal specification and rapid prototyping. *IEEE Transactions on Software Engineering*, SE-12, 2, 241-250.

[Hetzel 1984]     Hetzel, W. (1984). *The complete guide to software testing*. London: Collins.

[Hoare 1985]      Hoare, C. A. R. (1985). *Communicating sequential processes*. Englewood Cliffs, NJ: Prentice-Hall International.

[IBM/1]           IBM Systems Development Division Report TR 21.572.
[IBM/2]           IBM. *Estimating application development projects*. IBM report SR20-73333.

114

[ISDOS 1981]     ISDOS Project (1981). *PSL/PSA - user's reference manual*. Ann Arbor, Mich.: University of Michigan.

[Jackson 1983]     Jackson, M. A. (1983). *System Development*. Englewood Cliffs, NJ: Prentice-Hall.

[Jones 1980]     Jones, C. B. (1980). *Software development: a rigorous approach*. London: Prentice-Hall.

[Jones 1986]     Jones, C. B. (1986). *Systematic software development using VDM*. London: Prentice-Hall (UK).

[Kemmerer 1985]     Kemmerer, R. A. (1985). Testing formal specifications to detect design errors. *IEEE Transactions on Software Engineering*, **SE-11**, 1, 32-43.

[McCabe 1976]     McCabe, T. J. (1976). A complexity measure. *IEEE Transactions on Software Engineering*, **SE-2**, 308-320.

[McCabe 1985]     McCabe, T. J., & Schulmeyer, G. G. (1985). System testing aided by Structured Analysis: a practical experience. *IEEE Transactions on Software Engineering*, **SE-11**, 9, 917-921.

[Milner 1980]     Milner, R. (1980). *A calculus of communicating systems*. Springer Verlag, Lecture Notes on Computer Science, **92**. Berlin: Springer Verlag.

[Mullery 1979]     Mullery, G. P. (1979). CORE - a method for controlled requirement specification. In *Proceedings of the 4th International Conference on Software Engineering*, pp126-135. New York: IEEE Computer Society Press.

[Myers 1978]     Myers, G. J. (1978). *Composite/structured design*. New York: Van Nostrand Reinhold.

[Myers 1979]     Myers, G. J. (1979). *The art of software testing*. London: Wiley.

[NCC 1984]     NCC and DTI. (1984). *The STARTS Guide*. Manchester, England: NCC. {Note: a revision of this guide to tools was, at the time of writing, planned for 1987.}

[Panzl 1978]     Panzl, D. J. (1978). *Automatic software test drivers*. Computer, **11**, April, 44-50.

[Parnas 1985]     Parnas, D. L., & Weiss, D. M. (1985). Active design reviews: principles and practices. In *Proceedings of the 8th International Conference on Software Engineering*, pp132-136. New York: IEEE Computer Society Press.

[Peterson 1981]     Peterson, J. L. (1981). *Petri net theory and the modelling of systems*. Englewood Cliffs, N.J.: Prentice-Hall.

[Popek 1977]       Popek, G. J., Horning, J. J., Lampson, B. W., Mitchell, J. G., & London, R. L. (1977). Notes on the design of Euclid. *ACM SIGPLAN Notices*, **12**, 3, 11-18.

[Putnam 1978]      Putnam, L. H. (1978). A general empirical solution to the macro software sizing and estimating problem. *IEEE Transactions on Software Engineering*, **SE-4**, 345-361.

[Quirk 1977]       Quirk, W. J., & Gilbert, R. (1977). *The formal specification of requirements of complex realtime systems.* UKAEA report AERE-R8602. Harwell: UKAEA.

[Quirk 1978]       Quirk, W. J. (1978). *The automatic analysis of formal real-time system specifications.* UKAEA report AERE-R9046. Harwell: UKAEA.

[Rapps 1985]       Rapps, S., & Weyuker, E. J. (1985) Selecting software test data using data flow information. *IEEE Transactions on Software Engineering*, **SE-11**, 4, 367-375.

[Richardson 1985]  Richardson, D. J., & Clarke, L. A. (1985) Partition analysis: a method combining testing and verification. *IEEE Transactions for Software Engineering*, **SE-11**, 12, 1477-1490.

[Ross 1977]        Ross, D. T. (1977). Structured Analysis (SA): A language for communicating ideas. *IEEE Transactions on Software Engineering*, **SE-3**, 16-34.

[Salter 1976]      Salter, K. G. (1976). A methodology for decomposing system requirements into data processing requirements. In *Proceedings of the 2nd International Conference on Software Engineering*, pp91-101. New York: IEEE Computer Society Press.

[Stevens 1974]     Stevens, W. P., Myers, G. J., & Constantine, L. L. (1974). Structured design. *IBM Systems Journal*, **13**, 115-139.

[Sufrin 1985]      Sufrin, B. A., Sørensen, I. H., Morgan, C. C., & Hayes, I. J. (1985). *Notes for a Z Handbook.* Oxford University Programming Research Group internal report.

[Wasserman 1986]   Wasserman, A. I., Pircher, P. A., Shewmake, D. T., & Kersten, M. L. (1986). Developing interactive information systems with the User Software Engineering Methodology. *IEEE Transactions on Software Engineering*, **SE-12**, 2, 326-345.

[Weyuker 1980]     Weyuker, E. J., & Ostrand, T. J. (1980). Theories of program testing and the application of revealing subdomains. *IEEE Transactions on Software Engineering*, **SE-6**, 236-246.

[Woodward 1980]   Woodward, M. R., Hedley, D., & Hennell, M. A.   (1980).
Experience with path analysis and testing of programs. *IEEE
Transactions on Software Engineering*, **SE-6**, 278-286.

[Yourdon 1979]   Yourdon, E. (1979). *Structured walkthroughs*. New York:
Yourdon Press.

# Index

Page numbers in boldface represent the main entry for a topic.

**A**

| | page |
|---|---|
| Acceptance Testing | 10,**54** |
| Acceptance Test Plan | 8,10,**54**,56 |
| Ada | 49,64,89 |
| animation | 18 |
| - of the Requirements Expression | 38 |
| - of the System Specification | 43 |
| APL | 49 |
| assemblage | 70 |
| audit trail | 21 |

**B**

| | |
|---|---|
| black-box testing | **15**,55,71,79,82,83,97 |
| bottom-up testing | 109 |
| boundary-value analysis | 80,98 |
| budget for testing | 23 |

**C**

| | |
|---|---|
| C | 49 |
| cause-effect graphing | 80,98 |
| CCS | 48,53 |
| change control | 20 |
| COBOL | 49 |
| COCOMO | 66 |
| coded unit | see *module* |
| coding errors | 105 |
| cohesion | 90 |
| compatibility testing | 85 |
| completeness | |
| - of Requirements Expression | 32 |
| - of System Specification | 50 |
| - of System Design Specification | 63 |
| - of Integration Test Specification | 78 |

component 70
concordance 42
condition coverage 101
configuration management **19,72**
consistency verification 13
- of Requirements Expression 33
- of System Specification 42
- of System Design Specification 61,64
- of Integration Test Specification 75,78
control flow analysis 106
CORE 50,53
correctness of the Requirements Expression 52
coupling 91
coverage
- criterion 79,99 *et seq*
- measure 99
cross-reference generator 42
CSP 48,53
cyclomatic number 112

## D

data collection 26 *et seq*
data dictionary 43,64
decision coverage 101
deliverable 5
Delivered System **8,29,54**
demonstrative testing 82
Design by Objectives 35,36,46
design-directed testing 99
development phase 7
dry running 103
dual programming 110
dynamic data flow analysis 102
dynamic testing 13,20

## E

education 22
end product 5
equivalence partitioning 52,80,98
error analysis 112
error exit testing 83
error guessing 81,99
Euclid 48

## F

| | |
|---|---|
| Fagan Inspection | 39,63,94,104 |
| fault | |
| - diagnosis | 111 |
| - management | 4 |
| feasibility | |
| - of Requirements Expression | 35 |
| - of System Specification | 45 |
| - of System Design Specification | 65 |
| - of Unit Test Plan | 75 |
| Finite State Machines | 43,48,49,53,64 |
| flow analysis | 107 |
| flow graph | 100 |
| formal methods | 48,96 |
| Fourth Generation Language/Tool | 49 |

## G

| | |
|---|---|
| glossary | 34,42,43 |
| Gypsy | 48 |

## H

| | |
|---|---|
| help information testing | 83 |

## I

| | |
|---|---|
| implementation activity | 8 |
| Ina Jo | 48,53 |
| infeasible path | 106 |
| information flow analysis | 107 |
| information hiding | 91 |
| installation testing | 86 |
| integration testing | 10,43,78,79 |
| Integration Test Plan | 8,10,69,71,73 |
| Integration Test Specification | 71,73,75 |
| interviewing for the Requirements Expression | 38 |
| investigatory testing | 82 |

## J

| | |
|---|---|
| JSD | 59 |
| JSP | 1 |

## L

| | |
|---|---|
| language of the System Specification | 52 |
| LCSAJ | 102 |

life-cycle                                    6
- benefits of                                65
- costs of                                   65
LISP                                         49
limit testing                                84
litigation                                23,24

## M

MacCadd                                      53
maintenance potential testing                86
manual procedures testing                    86
MASCOT                                       79
**me too**                                   49
metrics                                      69
moderator                                    38
Modula-2                                     89
modularity                                   92
module                                    11,70
- code                                       89
- cohesion                                   90
- coupling                                   91
- design                                     11
- documentation                             96
- size                                       93
Module Specification              11,12,89,109
mutation analysis                           111

## O

OBJ                                          53
object oriented design                       59

## P

partition analysis                         108
PDL/81                                       53
performance                               81,85
Petri Net                                    48
pilot system                             **18,69**
predictability of a module                   95
project plan                                 18
Prolog                                       49
proof of a specification                     48
prototyping                      18,45,47,49,66
PSL                                          53

## Q

Quality Assurance                                    112

## R

random testing                                       110
RE                              see *Requirements Expression*
record-keeping                                     21,27
recovery testing                                      85
referability
- of Requirements Expression                          37
- of System Specification                             44
Reference Manual                                      82
regression testing                                    85
relevance of the System Specification                 51
reliability                                        81,85
requirement                                          31
Requirements Analysis                                10
requirements-directed testing                         97
Requirements Expression                        10,12,29
- checklists for                                      39
- interviewing for                                    38
revealing subdomains                                 102
review
- of Requirements Expression                          38
- of System Design Specification                      68
- of Module Specification                             94
RML                                               48,53
RSL                                                  53

## S

SADT                                                 53
SA Tools                                             53
security testing                                      85
semi-formal methods                                    1
SDS                          see *System Design Specification*
simulation                                           69
Software Data Library                                26
Software through Pictures                            53
SPADE                                            89,106
SPECIF                                               53
specification activity                                8
SPECK                                                49
SS                              see *System Specification*
SSADM                                           1,50,59
statement coverage                                   99

static analysis                                          89,106
- of data flow                                              106
static testing                                            11,20
stimulus/response pairs                                      54
storage testing                                             86
stress testing                                              84
structure chart generator                                  109
Structured Analysis                                      53,83
Structured Architect                                        53
Structured Design                                           79
Structured English                                          53
Structured Walkthrough                                39,63,103
stub                                                       109
symbolic execution                                         107
system design                                            10,59
System Design Specification                  10,11,12,60,88
System for Trial                                      29,53,60
System Specification                            10,12,29,89
- qualification, validation and testing of                 41
- testing system attributes                                56
- testing system constraints                               55
- testing system functions                                 54
system specification (act of)                              10
system testing                                          10,82

*T*

test
- effectiveness                                        23,111
- harness                                                  109
- log                                                       24
- management                                               24
- planning                                                 24
- software                                                 79
testability                                                16
- of a Module Specification                                93
- of a Requirements Expression                             36
- of a System Design Specification                         66
- of a System Specification                                44
Test Plan                                            13,16,24
tool support                                                3
top-down testing                                          109
traceability                                               21

## U

| | |
|---|---|
| unit testing | 11,89,103 |
| Unit Test Plan | 8,11,89,97,109 |
| user | 31 |
| User Guide | 82 |
| user information testing | 87 |
| User Software Engineering | 49 |
| User Trial Plan | 8 |

## V

| | |
|---|---|
| validation | 17 |
| - of the System Specification | 46 *et seq* |
| VDM | 1,48,53,63,94,96 |
| verification | 17 |
| - of code | 109 |
| version control | 21 |
| volume testing | 84 |

## W

| | |
|---|---|
| waterfall model | 6 |
| white-box testing | **15**,79,99 |

## Z

| | |
|---|---|
| Z | 1,48,53,63,96,98 |